# An Angel Whispered

The Wisdom & Practice
of Happiness

with love,
Patty

# An Angel Whispered

## The Wisdom & Practice of Happiness

### Patricia Tashiro

BOOKS

Winchester, UK
Washington, USA

With gratitude, to my teacher, Giziben,
an inspiring seeker of truth who has dedicated her life
to the service of others.

First published by O-Books, 2010
O-Books is an imprint of John Hunt Publishing Ltd., Laurel House, Station Approach,
Alresford, Hants, SO24 9JH, UK
office1@o-books.net
www.o-books.com

For distributor details and how to order please visit the 'Ordering' section on our website.

Text copyright: Patricia Tashiro 2010

ISBN: 978 1 84694 428 4

Design: Stuart Davies

Printed in the UK by CPI Antony Rowe
Printed in the USA by Offset Paperback Mfrs, Inc

We operate a distinctive and ethical publishing philosophy in all
areas of our business, from our global network of authors to
production and worldwide distribution.

# CONTENTS

# The Angel Arrives

My search for answers began in January 1997. Within the next six months I was going to get my master's degree, get married, move back to Asia, and find a job. In the midst of making these big life changes, like many people, I started to ask questions, like: "What am I doing?" "What *should* I be doing?" And ultimately, "What is my purpose in life?"

I searched for the answers to my questions in books. I read all sorts of self-discovery books to try to find my purpose in life. Thinking back now, I see that I was searching for what I was meant to be *doing* rather than trying to figure out who I was meant to *be*. Of course, now I realize the *doing* does not matter nearly as much as the *being*. And, in fact, we ought to be in a state of *being* no matter what we are *doing*.

Fortunately, many of the books I read recommended keeping a journal as a way to find your purpose. I soon found that the *doing* met the *being* when I was writing. When I was alone with a spiral notebook and a pen, I could get into a state where I felt my soul was speaking through the ink of my pen. And on some occasions, I felt I could hear the whispers of God. These were glorious moments, and so I wrote and wrote and wrote.

While writing, I questioned why things were the way they were. But more importantly, I wondered how they could be different. I soon found that at the heart of all of my writings was the belief that one person could make a difference. And then a shift in awareness, a heightened sense of consciousness, in even a few people, would change the world. I longed to see this shift, to see people *doing* in a different way.

Of course, the subtext of this was that the *different way* people had to do things was actually *my way*. The implication being *my way* was the *better* – or dare I say – *best way*. And so this became my unspoken purpose: to write a book that would somehow, in some way, inspire people to see things in a *different way* and therefore do in a *different way*, which was, of course, *my way*. You can probably guess where this is heading.

After writing numerous drafts of different books, by June 2004, I came to the realization that everything I had written fell far short of the mark. Worse yet, in looking at the state of the world, it seemed as if the situation was becoming worse. There seemed to be more conflict, more corruption, and more people suffering from a lack of food and water, not to mention all of the people who seemed to have everything, but felt as though they had nothing.

It was at this time, when I was feeling a bit disheartened, that I saw an advertisement for a talk by Dadi Janki, one of the leaders and founders of The Brahma Kumaris World Spiritual University (www.bkwsu.org). I had never heard of The Spiritual University or Dadi Janki, but I decided to attend and find out more.

I then learned The Spiritual University was founded in India in 1937 and had since grown to become a global organization. Now it has over 8,500 centers in 130 countries. It works on all levels of society to create positive change and, because of this, it has been awarded seven UN Peace Messenger Awards. All classes and courses were – and continue to be – offered for free, as a service to the community.

Even now, years later, I still remember that day and some of what Dadi Janki said during the talk. One piece of wisdom that resonated with me was that "we spend our lives filling our heads with knowledge, but if our hearts are empty, how can we be of any use to humanity?"

At the time I felt as if my heart was one tablespoon short of empty. And so I started attending classes at The Spiritual

University in London on a regular basis. There, I met my teacher, Gizi Pruthi.

In the first few lectures I attended, Giziben spoke so directly about so many things I had been exploring in my writings that I felt it was too much to be a coincidence. It was as if she had somehow read what I had written and was either filling in the holes or guiding me when I had gone astray. In some cases she confirmed my beliefs, noting that one person does indeed have the capacity to make a difference, to change the world. And in other cases, she corrected me, pointing out that if I really wanted to change the world I had to change *myself* – not convince others to change themselves.

And so this became my purpose in life – to change myself. To do this, I threw myself into my studies at The Spiritual University. And it was there, studying under Giziben, that my questions about life, death, God, and everything in between, were answered. It was a relief for things to finally make sense, and to know what I was meant to do and be.

As soon as I began to feel a shift within myself, I wished everyone I had ever known, and had never known, could have access to what I was learning. But how could I do it? How could I begin to convey an ocean of wisdom in the drop of a book? I struggled with this for some time. Then, while meditating one afternoon, the first two lines of a poem came to me:

*An angel whispered in my ear,*
*Words of wisdom I had longed to hear.*

I wrote them down and then just kept writing and writing and writing. The next thing I knew I had written a 10,000 word poem.

Soon after I finished it, my teacher went to lecture abroad and asked me to fill in for her in a few of her regular classes while she was away. I presented the poem, along with some explanations and anecdotes and received requests for copies of it. And so it seemed to me that the poem, along with some explanatory notes and quotes on each topic, was the way to share what I had learned.

With this said, it is with great hesitation that I share what I have learned so far, as I am still a student, who has yet to be tested by life, and not a teacher. Although I know I have made many strides, I also know I have just started on this journey, a journey that will take the rest of my life. And may it be a long life, as I still have so much to learn!

But I also know the process of writing and rewriting – and ultimately sharing – will help me more deeply understand, accept, and practice all I have learned.

This book highlights some of the points of wisdom and practice that have been most helpful to me so far and does not attempt to convey all that is shared by my teacher or by The Spiritual University. Everything I share comes from my experience and is not an official view of The Spiritual University's teachings.

As for the structure of the book, Part One focuses on the Wisdom of Happiness and describes how I am making an effort to shift my thinking to restore my peace of mind. Part Two focuses on the Practice of Happiness, which describes how I am shifting the way I think, speak, and act so I can bring love back into my heart.

My teacher often says happiness is experienced when you have peace of mind and love in your heart. And for me, the doing and being come together when I have peace of mind and love in my heart and experience happiness.

In the end, I hope this book answers at least some of your questions and helps you on your path to becoming who you are meant to be. And then together – quietly, peacefully, and with love – in our doing and being, we *will* make a difference, not by changing others, but by changing ourselves. With that, let the angel arrive:

An angel whispered in my ear,
Words of wisdom I had longed to hear.

For years, many questions plagued my mind.
I searched for answers, but did not find.

Most of my questions began with "Why?"
That awful word that makes the heart cry.

So I said to the heavens, "I want to know.
Please just tell me, so I won't feel low."

In that moment, the angel came,
A blaze of light, without a name.

"Hello, Sweet Child, feel free to ask.
To answer you is my sole task."

In her presence came a burst of hope.
I felt relief from the words she spoke.

But what to ask? Where should I start?
With the questions in my head? Or the ache in my heart?

She smiled and gave me a little wink.
"Why not start with the way you think?

What you think determines how you feel.
If your mind's at peace, your heart will heal."

# PART ONE

## The Wisdom of Happiness:

## Restoring Peace of Mind

# Why Do We Suffer? Why Is There Pain?

"Okay, so... why do we suffer? Why is there pain?
It seems there's no point. There's nothing to gain."

"First, I must say, to be very clear,
Pain and suffering are different, my dear.

Pain is of the body, which is made up of matter.
It's what you feel when you fall off a ladder.

Suffering, however, happens up in the mind,
When your thoughts are unhappy or simply unkind.

Pain is inevitable, from which there's no escape.
But suffering is optional; it's from the thoughts you create."

Was suffering optional? This I couldn't believe.
I thought it was inevitable, that it was guaranteed.

If it were an option, who would make this choice?
Don't most people prefer to laugh and rejoice?

I didn't want to interrupt, but I had to ask,
"Could you please explain what you just said last?"

"Yes, of course, I am happy to oblige.
This is the role of a spiritual guide.

## Chapter I

Suffering occurs when you think in a wrong way,
You're living in the past or fearing the next day.

In some way or another, you're clinging or resisting.
You're dreading what is, when you ought to be shifting.

When you're hanging on, suffering tells you to let go.
It gives you a signal that's important to know.

But if you do not listen, then suffering is guaranteed.
You need to think another way to make yourself free.

So although suffering is optional, it's a necessary low,
To push you to change, so you can grow."

I remember the first time I heard my teacher say, "Suffering is optional." It was such an incredible statement. I wanted to know how. How on earth could suffering be optional?

Although I had not suffered much in my life, I certainly wanted to know how I could opt out of any future suffering. For me, suffering was inevitable; it was guaranteed. It was something to avoid for as long as possible; and then when it came, something to just endure until it passed. It was not optional. There was no choice involved.

It was not until I learned that our thoughts make us suffer, and not what is actually happening around us, that I began to see how suffering could be optional. Since we create our thoughts, we determine whether we suffer or not depending on the thoughts we create.

For this to work, however, we need to think in a new way about who we are, who God is, and why things happen. In the absence of being given an alternative way to think about life and why things happen, we will continue to suffer. And certainly, every time I revert to my old ways of thinking, I open myself up to suffering. It is a daily practice – a re-training of the heart and mind – that will take a lifetime.

Although the journey will take a lifetime, the good news is that it does not take that long to see a change within. For me, after a few months I felt as if a spark of hope had been reignited. For others, who come in the midst of facing great challenges, it may take a little longer. With this said, I have been inspired by some students who have endured incredible hardships and through their effort have transformed their lives and reduced their suffering.

In exploring suffering, I now realize that we do not suffer only when things go wrong, but we can also suffer when things go well. We suffer every time we fear we will lose whatever it is we have. We create fear when we think "What if..." and imagine something grim happening to a loved one, our health, our wealth, or even to the environment. And fear cannot be separated from suffering.

My teacher has said, "If you look at saints and sages, they do not suffer. No matter what they face – even physical pain – they do not suffer. This is because they are said to be 'friendly with the inevitable.' They do not resist what is. They do not wish for things to be any different than they are. They are in a state of acceptance and of fullness, which enables them to be in a state of love." At every moment, they know what they are meant to do and be.

*"Suffering is necessary until you realize suffering is no longer necessary."*
Buddha

# Why Are We Here? What Is Our Purpose?

"But grow into what? Why are we here?
What is our purpose? Please make it clear."

"The answer is simple. You may think it's sappy.
But the hard truth is, you are meant to be happy.

Whatever you do, wherever you go,
Whomever you meet, you mustn't feel low.

To be able to do this, two things you must find:
Love in your heart and peace in your mind.

If you can do this and add these two together,
Happiness is yours, no matter the weather.

So that is your purpose, that is your calling,
To learn to be happy without any stalling."

I paused for a second. What had I heard?
Learn to be happy? It sounded absurd.

I said, "Are you kidding? Are you telling a joke?
The world is on fire. It's going up in smoke.

Families are fighting and countries seek to kill.
People are starving and countless are ill.

How can I be happy? How can I smile?
The world's in such a state, every square mile."

"I hear what you're saying. It all seems unfair.
But listen to your words. Your answer is there.

If people were happy to the center of their core,
Would there be conflict? Would there be war?

While you may accept this, as it's simple to see,
I'll tell you something else, you may not believe.

There would be no hunger, not one empty plate.
People wouldn't become ill, that wouldn't be their fate."

"Is that so? I would like to accept.
But what if others decide to reject?

What if I became happy and no one else did?"
To that she replied, "What's the alternative?

You can get angry and you can get mad.
Or you can sulk and feel really sad.

It's your choice. It's up to you.
You can decide what you want to do.

But whatever you choose, why not be wise?
Why would you fall down, when you can rise?

Don't you think people follow? Go along with the group?
Why not lead people to stand and not ever to stoop?

It was once said, 'Be the change you wish to see,'
So this is the advice I give unto thee.

Unfortunately most people don't try to change the self.
Instead they try hard to change everyone else!

This causes pain and makes people suffer.
The harder they try it only becomes tougher.

Why not do what you can to make yourself better?
This will heal the world, like a powerful love letter."

In a talk I attended one evening, the speaker said, "If you ask most people, 'What is your purpose in life?' They don't have an answer. And yet, they're very busy. Busy working towards what, they don't know, but they're very busy."

This insight resonated with me when I heard it because of my own search for meaning and purpose. Until I could answer this question, I felt like I was drifting, a rudderless boat, pulled by the whims and waves of others. But when I could answer this question – although the answer has changed over the years, then all of a sudden, my time, money, and energy were channeled toward that purpose.

When I was studying for my master's degree in international relations, people often joked that if you asked the students there about their purpose in life, they would say one of three things: to rule the world, own the world, or save the world. I fell firmly into the third camp and lived my life accordingly. I became a vegetarian because it was easier on the environment. I perspired in the summer and froze in the winter to conserve energy. I supported all of the "right" candidates and "right" causes, and, as I mentioned before, I tried to write the "right" book to make everything "right" in the world.

So, it came as a shock to me to hear that our purpose is to be happy. To be honest, the first time I heard this I thought, "What does happiness have to do with anything?" Of course, I was soon to find out that happiness had everything to do with everything.

But from my perspective at the time I thought, "Once we stop these people from killing each other, give those people food and medicine, save that patch of earth, protect this endangered species, and on and on and on... then we can be happy. But not a minute before then." Happiness seemed to me to be a trite external pursuit that I confused with pleasure. Therefore, it did not interest me, although I considered myself to be a fairly happy person.

Since then, I have realized that happiness is an essential ingredient for human life. And, it is not an external pursuit at all, although it has been billed as this. It has nothing to do with pleasure, which is when we take our "happiness" from the outside and bring it in through the senses. This sort of "happiness" depends on everything on the outside – particularly what other people say or do.

Happiness is actually an internal pursuit and has nothing to do with pleasure. It is experienced when we can bring peace into our minds and feel love in our hearts. It is a deep state of contentment when we do not need anything from anyone. When we can do this, and are completely content, we want the best for ourselves and everyone. Then we become truly generous, not in terms of giving other people our money, but in terms of giving other people permission to be who they are. In this state, we give everyone the gift they long for, which is the feeling of being accepted and having a sense of belonging.

I soon realized, as Brahma Baba, the founder of The Spiritual University, said, "People only hurt other people when they are unhappy." When we cannot bear the pain within, we seek to release it and, inevitably, someone is hurt. When we are happy, we cannot harm the self or others. It would disturb our minds and shut down our hearts, which is the last thing we would want to do. All we would want is to stay in a state of bliss.

Knowing this, I now realize I had it backwards. I thought we needed to fix everything *out there* so we could be happy *inside*. But in fact, we cannot fix anything out there until we are happy on the inside. When we are not happy, whatever we do will be tainted by an agenda to make the self feel better. We may tell ourselves we are doing something for someone else, but in truth, we are only trying to make ourselves feel better. This is not serving others; it is serving the self.

As I said earlier, my hidden agenda in my writing was to try to convince others to do things *my way*, which is a recipe for suffering. My teacher has said, "People will pick up on your agenda to change them and then they will resist you. In time, you will become frustrated that things are not progressing the way you planned and then you will begin to feel angry. And then a passion will be born in you to change other people and situations so that you can be happy. But passion is just a mask for anger. And while short-term gains can be made through anger and intimidation, no lasting change will come from this. Transformation only occurs when there is a shift in our hearts and minds."

Being happy does not mean not taking any action. We are not meant to be passive, cold, unengaged, or indifferent. Being happy simply means we are full, completely content, and then in that state of fullness, we do whatever it is we need to do. This contrasts with what I used to do, which was to do something to fill myself up, to make myself feel better.

In truth, we all know the wisdom of the ripple effect, that we have the capacity to affect others positively and negatively. We know a simple gesture we make toward someone, be it friendly or unfriendly, has the capacity to change the trajectory of that person's day, or even his or her life. In light of this, we must check ourselves and make sure our thoughts, words, and deeds are of the highest standard.

While Mahatma Gandhi's quote, "You must be the change you wish to see in the world," always resonated with me, I never truly practiced this wisdom before coming to The Spiritual University. Although I would have said that I wanted a peaceful, loving world, I felt quite right in dividing the world into those who were good and those who were not. I was quick to judge and condemn those who did not do as I would have wanted them to do. But in this state, there was not peace in my mind or love in my heart.

And even though I had been a student of international relations, I did not have the wisdom to live up to the preamble of the constitution of UNESCO, which states: "Since wars begin in the minds of men, it is in the minds of men that the defences of peace must be constructed." I can see now that if we want peace in our world, then we must learn how to bring peace into our minds. Only then can we find happiness within and hope to forge loving harmonious relationships with others.

*"I believe that the very purpose of our life is to seek happiness. That is clear. Whether one believes in religion or not, whether one believes in this religion or that religion, we are all seeking something better in life. So, I think, the very motion of our life is towards happiness..."*
   Dalai Lama

# How Can I Be Happy
# When Life Is So Unfair?

"But how can I be happy, when life is so unfair?
When others do wrong, it's more than I can bear."

"I know you may think what they did is a shame.
And now you feel miserable, so they are to blame.

But let me tell you a secret, that is really true,
The way that you feel is solely because of you.

You had a thought they should act a certain way,
But they did something different and you had no say.

So who is to blame for you taking sorrow?
And who is at fault when you seek revenge tomorrow?

Is it the other, who didn't do as you please?
Or is it you, whose thoughts were diseased?

The other's capacity you failed to consider.
This was the problem. This made you bitter.

So when you feel you're starting to sink,
Stop and ask yourself, 'What did I think?

What did I expect that the other failed to do?'
But don't examine the other, just look at you.

In one way or another your thoughts were faulty,
This was the problem. This made your tears salty!"

Since I did not know what happiness was or how it was created, mine ebbed and flowed according to what was happening around me. While watching the news, I would become happy with a hopeful story, but then become sad with news of the latest terrorist attack or natural disaster.

In the presence of others, I would feel good when I was around someone who was happy, positive, and treated me well, but then feel badly when someone was angry, sulking, or unkind. My happiness was not my own. For the most part, happiness was something I took from the outside and brought inside.

And so I lived my life thinking that other people and situations had the capacity to make me feel. In the face of injustice or unkindness, I thought whoever had done wrong in my eyes was to blame for my unhappiness. It was *the other person* who made me feel badly. So, it was news to me to learn that no one had the capacity to make me feel. No one had ever disappointed, insulted, or hurt me. Nor had anyone ever made me angry. When I first heard this I thought, "If you think that's true then you haven't been watching very closely!"

But I soon learned, as cognitive and positive psychologists also assert, that we feel according to the thoughts we have. We only feel disappointed, insulted, hurt, or angry when someone has not done as we wished. We had a thought – an expectation or desire – that someone should act a certain way, and he or she failed to do so. This is what made us lose our happiness – our expectation – not what the other person actually said or did. And so we live our lives expecting people to sustain us by acting according to how we need them to act so we can be happy. And when they do not, we lose our happiness.

My teacher has said, "It's as if we ask an apple merchant for oranges. And then when we're given apples, we're upset. But people don't always have what we're looking for. If they could have given us what we wanted, they would have done so, but they just didn't have it to give. So don't ask people to give you love, if they have had a life that has filled them with anger. They don't have any love to give. They would give it to you if they could, but they just can't. Instead, take responsibility for yourself and don't blame others for not giving you what you wanted. Recognize you misjudged their capacity and learn to give yourself what you require."

This gem of wisdom has restored my happiness on countless occasions. Whenever I lose my happiness and think someone else was to blame, I ask myself, "What was I looking to take – love, respect, appreciation, or regard – that the other failed to give me?"

As soon as I know the answer, I take responsibility for myself. Why was I asking someone else to give me something that I need to learn to give myself? Then I internally thank the other for not giving me what I wanted, as that person is teaching me how to generate true happiness, which comes from within, rather than taking it from the outside.

This means, of course, that we have to be able to create the "right" thoughts in all circumstances with all people, if we are to sustain our own happiness. We need to embrace a new way of thinking about anything – be it death, injustice, or God – that has the capacity to take away our happiness.

*"I've learned from experience that the greater part of our happiness or misery depends on our dispositions and not on our circumstances."*
Martha Washington

# Why Must We Die?

"So ask me your next question. You wanted to know why."
I did not hesitate, "Tell me, why must we die?"

It took just a moment before she paused and smiled.
Then she quietly said, "You never die, my sweet child."

Then *I* paused and pondered, was silent and perplexed.
I wondered for a second if I should be vexed.

And then the angel said, "Let me open the curtain of illusion.
If you can get this, you can end this dreadful delusion.

Everyone has a body that is born and that will die.
In between is called life. This is truth, not a lie.

But what drives this body? What makes it move?
What makes it think? What makes it groove?

A powerful energy, the light of the soul.
This divine being has a very simple goal:

To express and experience is what it comes to do.
Sadly it becomes lost under the guise of *you*.

You begin to think the body is who you are,
But this is not true. It's the soul who is the star.

The soul is eternal. It knows not birth or death.
It is metaphysical and does not take in breath.

The body, however, will surely decay.
It's made up of matter, for long it can't stay.

When a soul leaves a body, you say that it's dead.
But the soul lives on. This is what's left unsaid.

It had to move on, on that exact date.
Not one second too early or one second too late.

If you want to be happy, you must remember this,
You're not a mortal body, but a soul filled with bliss."

If there were a time in my life when I suffered, it was when a high school friend, who was 18 years old, died of cancer. At 18, you are supposed to be starting your life, taking your hopes and dreams with you to university, not thinking about – let alone facing – death. And yet every day that summer, the thought of death and the fear of losing my friend was with me. Every day I wondered, "Why? Why is this happening? Why him? Why me? Why now?"

No one could answer my questions, at least not to my satisfaction. Of course, I was told this was a part of "God's plan" and that sometimes His plan is "beyond our comprehension." But I did not believe this or accept it. Even though I prayed to God to spare my friend, and even threatened Him, I did not believe God played us like chess pieces, healing some people and leaving others to die.

I now see that the explanation that it was God's will could be helpful if it stopped the questions and helped me move into acceptance. But I did not accept this explanation and so I continued to resist what was, which only deepened and prolonged my suffering.

I should add that if my teacher had suddenly come to me during the dark days of that summer and shared all the teachings I have learned, I probably would not have been able to free myself from suffering. This is because, as my teacher has observed, it is very hard to accept help and heal in the midst of suffering. Although we must try, sometimes we have to wait until the worst has passed. Then, when the pain is not so intense, we can learn what we must from what happened so we will not suffer as deeply the next time.

With this said, even today, I do not think I would be free from suffering if faced with losing a loved one. I only hope I would be able to move through the grief more quickly than before.

Thinking back now, when my friend died I believed his soul went to heaven and that he was with God. And yet I still cried. To this I have heard my teacher say, "If you believe your loved one has gone to heaven, then why are you crying? You should be delighted your loved one has left this world of pain and suffering and is in bliss with God." Of course, the answer to this is that I wanted my friend with me, not God, even if this world were filled with pain and suffering, I wanted him here to help sustain me and my happiness.

Now I see, as my teacher often says, that we never cry for others. We may think we cry for others, but really, we only cry for ourselves. I was not crying for him, but for me, for my loss, for my need to have him with me, and for my own fear of what was to become of me after I died. My tears came from my own needs, my own emptiness.

In truth, we are supposed to be able to sustain ourselves. If we can do this, then we can love and enjoy others while they are with us and then let them go when it is time for them to move on. We need to recognize that other souls come to us for a period of time and then move on when their time comes. It is as if we are riding on a train to a certain destination and various passengers will get on and off along the way. When they get on, we enjoy their company or learn what we must from them. But when they get off, we need to let them continue on their own journeys without clinging or resisting.

This capacity to sustain the self does not come from knowing about death, but from knowing about life. It comes from knowing who we are, that we are not mortal beings subject to the whims of fate, but eternal beings who have the capacity to determine the quality of every moment we have. It is only once we understand this and move into a state of acceptance that we can begin to become "friendly with the inevitable." But to do so, we must know who we are.

*"Death is not the greatest loss in life. The greatest loss is what dies inside us while we live."*
Norman Cousins

# 5

## Who Am I?

"I'm not sure I understand. So, in truth, we do not die?"
"Everything will become clear, if you simply ask, 'Who am I?'

The answer to *this* question you must come to know,
If you're to find true happiness and be free from feeling low."

"So tell me who I am. Fill in this gaping hole."
"I have already told you: you're not a body, but a soul."

"But I know I have a soul. This much I have been told.
And yet I still fear death and worry about becoming old."

"You said you *have* a soul. But this I didn't declare.
I said you *are* a soul. This is what I shared.

But what is a soul? A soul is a point of light.
It is a child of God that's filled with virtue and might.

Embedded within the soul is the memory of what it's known.
No two are the same, though they come from the same home.

Their home is up above, with God beyond this earth,
Although they come here and receive a body through birth.

Only in a body can a soul experience and express,
Depending on its memory, it'll be happiness or distress.

But please do not worry, all will become clear.
You will understand the more that you hear.

Know your nature's good, though you have a bit of greed.
The greatest irony is you already have what you need."

Hearing this piece of wisdom gave me a chill up my spine.
I wanted to know more, what was already mine.

"You spend your life looking for what you already have.
It's like you're riding in a car, but searching for a cab.

You search for peace in nature, in the woods or at the beach,
Sometimes you can feel it, but nature's not always in reach.

You search for love in others, you want it from other people.
As soon as you feel it, you run to the nearest steeple.

But peace isn't out there in a bush or a tree.
And love isn't found in the people you see.

Both are an experience that takes place in the mind.
If triggered from the outside, then you're in a bind.

Now you're dependent on something made of matter,
It could be a beautiful scene or someone else's pitter-patter.

But what if I told you, 'You *are* peace and love?'
Would this not give you the lightness of a dove?

For these you need not search, these virtues are in you.
But you are many more, not just these two.

You are purity, happiness, wisdom, and power.
You are the radiance and fragrance of a beautiful flower.

But this you don't believe. You've been told that you're less.
This falsehood you accept. Then everything becomes a mess.

I will admit, of course, the vices have taken root.
But I know, in a second, you could give them the boot.

If only you realized the vice of ego brings anger.
Attachment, lust and greed, put your happiness in danger.

You don't think you have love or peace within yourself.
So your ego quietly says, 'Take it from someone else.'

All the vices convince you what you need is out there,
So you search and you search for as long as you dare.

But you already *are* that for which you long.
If you'd just realize this, you'd sing a sweet song."

When I studied Japanese, it was said that first-year students would tell you they are fluent, but fifth-year students would tell you they have only just begun to learn. I believe this wisdom also applies to answering the question, "Who am I?"

When I first learned who I was, it seemed simple: I am a soul. I am a child of God. I am eternal. I am the embodiment of goodness. I *am* peace. I *am* love. And my home is beyond this world.

But as I started to explore the meaning of being a soul, I began to think I had barely grasped what it meant to be a soul. And then it did not seem so simple. I suspect once you really understand what it means to be a soul, then everything becomes quite simple again.

When I grew up, all I knew about souls was this:

1. I had a soul.
2. After I died, my soul would go to heaven, hell, or purgatory – that Catholic halfway house for souls.

Other than that, I knew nothing. But it was not until I understood what it meant to be a soul that everything began to make sense.

There are many analogies that clarify what it means to be a soul. One is that the soul is the driver while the body is the car. The soul drives the body, giving it directions, and the body does as the soul commands. Another analogy is that the soul is an actor and the body is the costume the actor wears. The soul is not the costume. It is merely playing a role – spouse, parent, child, sibling, employer or employee, of a certain race, nationality, and gender – but that is not *who it is*.

When we begin to think we are the body or identify with the roles we play, we begin to think we are a spouse, parent, or child, with certain physical characteristics, and then begin to act according to the conditioning associated with each role. When things do not happen according to our conditioning, we lose our happiness. So, rather than knowing who we are – souls playing a role – we begin to believe we are the roles we play. And believing we are something we are not is a recipe for unhappiness.

To begin to understand that the soul is separate from the body and is not the identity given by the body, it is helpful to think of accounts given by people who have had near death experiences. Many of these people, including children and adults from different cultures, religions, and nationalities, describe their souls separating from their bodies, floating up into a corner of a room, and looking down.

As a soul hovers above, looking down, who is it? What is it? Is it a mother or father or child or sibling? Is it male or female? Does it have a race, religion, or nationality? Is it rich or poor? Is it healthy or ill? It is none of these things. These are all ways we describe our bodies and the state of our bodies, which is not who we are.

My teacher describes the soul as an infinitesimal point of energy. Embedded within this point is the record of every thought, word, and deed of the soul while it has played its parts on earth. The original nature of the soul is divine and virtuous. Therefore, at our core, we are good, the embodiment of all of the virtues. The difference among us lies in the depth and strength of our virtues and the extent to which the vices have entered us. Happiness lies in uncovering and strengthening our virtues, while letting go of our vices.

If we are to use the virtues instead of the vices, we have to become familiar with them. I am still learning to recognize the vices and virtues in myself, so I will relate definitions my teacher has given. There are five main vices:

*Lust* is an intensified form of desire, of wanting to possess. It is not limited to physical lust, but also includes the desire for possessions, power, and people, as well as the desire for approval, appreciation, and acceptance. It arises out of comparison, which ignites attraction and stimulates all of the vices to awaken.

*Greed* and lust are closely connected, but subtly different. With lust there is an aspect of controlling others, but with greed, it is all about satisfying the self.

*Attachment* develops to whatever our happiness depends on. It is not only for what people do and do not give us, but also to our possessions, position, power, and certainly to our perspective.

*Ego* causes the most misery and is at the root of all suffering. It projects a false image of the self to enable us to take from outside. It identifies with external things and causes us to think in terms of *I* and *my*. Our egos are active whenever we think, "I am right."

*Anger* is a secondary vice that arises when one of the desires of the primary vices is not satisfied. Anger helps us make others behave in a way that suits us so we can return to happiness.

The key to happiness is using the virtues that lie latent within us, instead of the vices. There are five main virtues:

*Purity* comes when we stop thinking about other people, the past, or the future and start thinking about what we need to do now. Purity awakens all of the other virtues within us.

*Peace* is being non-violent in our thoughts, words, and deeds, with no resistance within us. Peace arises when we realize we already have everything we need. With peace, there is power.

*Love* allows other people to be who they are. Even though we may not agree with the choices or opinions of others, we accept them as they are, without wanting to change one morsel of them.

*Happiness* is experienced when we are not dependent on people, circumstances, or substances. We enjoy a wonderful interdependency with friends, family, colleagues, and neighbors, but have no expectations others must fulfill for us to maintain our happiness.

*Wisdom* emerges when there is no negativity within us and we can access the truth that lies latent within. With this deep inner wisdom, confusion and questions cease.

When we are coming from a place of virtue, we are free and light. Our relationships are no longer tainted by hidden agendas to receive love or respect from others. All fears and desires fade because our happiness depends on no one. This enables us to give freely of the self, without the slightest thought of receiving anything, like appreciation, approval, or acceptance, in return. In this state, we realize that we already have everything we need and need not search for anything.

It is only when we understand who we are, what a soul is,

and what its story is that we can begin to think in a way that allows us to experience who we are and to restore our happiness.

*"We are not human beings on a spiritual journey. We are spiritual beings on a human journey."*
Stephen R. Covey

# Why Do We Not Feel Whole?

"If we are goodness then why don't we feel whole?"
"Everything is explained by the story of the soul.

There once was a time when all souls were complete.
Virtue was their nature, so they did not compete.

But after many births, the soul becomes weak.
And then the experience starts to become bleak.

When you were full, you could sustain the self,
You enjoyed prosperity, and were always in good health.

Your happiness didn't depend on someone else's actions.
You were peaceful and loving, without any reactions.

The soul was so clean during this beautiful time.
But now souls have become dirty, so burdened with grime.

Because the soul becomes weaker, like a battery run down,
You forget you're a soul and identify with nouns!

Your sense of self comes from your religion and race.
Your happiness is tied to work and to seeing another's face.

Your belief of who you are comes from the body you have.
This makes you feel better, like a temporary salve.

When those with whom you identify do well or as you wish,
You feel so good and think you are in bliss.

When you're in good health and people recognize your name,
You feel such a boost, you don't register any pain.

But then surely it happens: things don't go your way.
Then your happiness falls and it's a very sad day.

It's easy to see what makes this occur.
When you look outside to try to feel secure.

I hesitate to say this, it may sound impertinent,
But you foolishly tie your happiness to what is impermanent.

Knowing a loss must occur, the mind creates fear,
So you think in a way that guarantees many tears.

You divide the world into two separate lots,
Those who are like you and those who are not.

For some you have love and a lot of compassion.
Others you dislike or even hate with a passion.

You're running on empty. Your virtues have gone.
The vices have taken over. Now everything goes wrong.

Instead of being a giver, which is what you're meant to be,
You turn into a taker and must grovel on your knees.

Others must sustain you and do as you desire.
If they do not, there will be tears or a fire.

Oh, what a tragedy, what a terrible loss.
You're no longer in charge. Everyone else is the boss!

This makes you suffer. This is the greatest curse.
Thinking you're not whole, you venture out and search.

Out there you can't find love, so inside you begin to hate.
And now you wonder why the world's in such a state."

When I began considering why things were the way they were,
the story of the fall of man was the only spiritual explanation I
had heard of for the state of the human condition. As the story
went, we were in our current condition because of choices made
by Adam and Eve, or by man in general, depending on what you
believed.

Looking at the result, with all the pain and suffering, it
seemed to me as though free choice were more of a curse than a
blessing. I saw it as a curse for two reasons. First, the fall was
always explained as if Adam and Eve had chosen and we had
inherited the consequences of those choices. So in fact, we had
not chosen at all. This made me wonder why I was paying for
what someone else had done. It did not seem right. It did not
seem fair.

And second, the fall was usually explained as if there were
no chance to ever stand up again. Once we had fallen, that was
it. Just by being born we were labelled sinners. And from that
moment on we were eternally doomed to suffer in life, with only
a chance of enjoying bliss in heaven after death. Again, this did
not seem right to me. Were we really meant to suffer in life? If
we truly had the power of choice, could we not just as easily
make choices to free us from our suffering?

While I finally just accepted that we were stuck with what
others had chosen, I did not accept that we were doomed to
suffer in life. I truly believed life could be different, if only we

chose differently. Therefore, much of my writings were about trying to inspire, convince, or cajole others to make new choices.

Of course, at that time I was not thinking *I* had to make new choices. I was fine – dare I say – perfect; everyone else had to change. This false thinking reveals just how far I had fallen. I was in such a state I could not see what I needed to do, but instead occupied my mind with what everyone else had to do.

But my standard of perfection was quite different from *true* perfection. *True* perfection is when our happiness does not depend on anyone or anything, when we can sustain ourselves no matter what. Anything short of that and there is room for improvement.

A story that illustrates how our happiness is not our own is one I heard from a Japanese businessman I met just once when I was living in Japan. He was quite candid and told me it was when he lived in New York that he realized he was prejudiced.

When Americans would ask him whether he was Korean or Chinese, he said a reaction would boil up within him. Indignantly he would reply, "No, I'm *Japanese*." Each time this occurred, his distaste for Americans grew.

Then one day it occurred to him that most Americans just did not know the difference among Asians, to them all Asians were the same. And then he wondered what the difference was and why he cared that Americans knew this. The answer was, of course, that he considered other nationalities to be lesser than his own and did not want to be identified with them.

Interestingly, he said that as soon as he realized he was prejudiced, it was as if his prejudice evaporated. From that moment on, he did not care what nationality people thought he was and he felt an affinity for other Asians and Americans that he had never felt before.

This story resonated with me because there have been many occasions in my own life when someone perceived me to be something I did not want to be seen as and I lost my happiness.

Now I know we lose our happiness when we try to project an image of the self – whether it is as an independent working woman or as a stay-at-home mom or something else – and others do not see us as we want to be seen. We are trying to take support from the roles our bodies play to boost ourselves up, but these supports regularly crumble and cause us to fall.

A more subtle way we lose our happiness is connected to our beliefs and the way we conduct ourselves. We tend to think that the way we think, believe, and act is better than other ways. We can inflate our sense of self by taking pride in being accurate, on time, reliable, frugal, moral, righteous, or in living simply. And we can take pride in what we do or in being a perfectionist. But then, when things do not happen as we hope, or we do not do as well as we think we could have done, we lose our happiness.

The litmus test I have learned for checking whether I am in the awareness of being a body or a soul is to ask myself how I am thinking about *I* and *my*. When I think I am a body I will think, "*I* am this profession, this nationality, this gender, this religion, this physique, and more subtly, this talented, this knowledgeable…" Everything associated with this *I* opens me up to feeling hurt, insulted, or disappointed, depending on the words and deeds of others. Or I will think in terms of possession, "This is *my* spouse, *my* child, *my* house, *my* car, *my* idea, *my* work, *my* creation…" And everything I think I possess opens me up to the fear of loss.

But as a soul, I simply think, "*I* am a peaceful soul." In this true awareness of *I*, I cannot be hurt, insulted, or disappointed. I am the embodiment of good qualities and virtues. And when I think *my*, all I think is, "This is *my* God, *my* Father." When I think in this way, I fear nothing. God is eternal and cannot be lost, broken, or stolen. In truth, a soul owns nothing and so it cannot lose anything. It comes into the world with nothing and will leave with nothing. So, to think I possess anything is a state of falsehood that simply breeds the fear of loss.

Of course, I have a duty to look after my loved ones, my body, and my possessions, but I cannot tie my happiness to them, for they are made of matter and cannot last forever. When I achieve this state, I will be able to love everyone purely, as there will be no fear left within me.

Over time I have come to believe the state of the human condition, both individually and collectively, *is* determined by free choice. While I rejected this notion before, as it was told in the context that we only live once, when I opened myself up to the idea of a soul living more than one life and the law of karma, I could see that I had chosen the circumstances I was in, both individually and collectively.

In truth, every thought, word, and deed we have had determines our state of being and the state of the world. As Buddha said:

*We are what we think.*
*All that we are arises with our thoughts.*
*With our thoughts, we make the world.*

When I realized this, I began to take responsibility for my state of being and the state of the world, and I started to do what I needed to do to improve myself.

And so it is true that free choice, which brought about the fall, can also enable us to ascend. *This is the blessing.* We are not cursed, doomed to suffer, but rather, we have the capacity to rise. Through the power of choice, we can choose our way out of suffering. When we do this, we choose our way back into paradise.

*"Knowledge of what is possible is the beginning of happiness."*
George Santayana

# Who Is God? What Does God Do?

"But what about God? We search for Him too.
Is He also within us? What exactly does He do?"

"No, He isn't in you. But I know what you've been told.
That He's in everything: plants, animals, and even gold.

But think about it, please. Could this be true?
If God were everywhere, would people feel blue?

Would humans ever do something that was wrong?
Or have pain and suffering to endure for so long?"

I said, "I don't think so. It doesn't sound right.
If God were in us, I don't think we would fight."

She replied with a smile, "This I knew that you'd know.
The God that we speak of doesn't have a foe.

But although He isn't *in* you, He can surely be *with* you.
So feel that you're one, but know that you're two.

Now ask me, 'Who is God?' This question you must pose."
I couldn't wait to hear, "Tell me everything you know."

"He is a point of light. He is the Supreme Soul.
He is loving and benevolent and only has one goal.

For you to learn to be happy at this difficult time,
So you won't be just human, but utterly divine."

"But this isn't what I've heard. What about God's will?
Doesn't God play a role when many are killed?

Who makes the earth rumble? Who makes it shake?
Who brings the tsunamis that turn cities into lakes?

Who takes our loved ones? Who takes them away?
If it isn't God, then why do we pray?"

"It is these false notions that cause people to suffer.
When they think that God has made their life tougher.

God doesn't play favorites. He doesn't pick and choose.
He doesn't say this one will win, and this one will lose.

It's not a surprise that some don't believe.
They don't know the truth and feel so deceived."

"Often it's said that He doesn't exist.
What do you reply to those who insist?"

"'If you don't believe in God, this is okay.
Just believe in goodness,' is all that I say.

But it's often quite funny, if you ask them why.
God is actually innocent; *man* has made them cry!

But in the absence of wisdom, it's a time of confusion.
So many suffer living under delusions."

## Chapter 7

I never really understood who God was or what He did. If asked, I would have said I believed in God, but beyond that, I did not know anything. I did not know why some prayers were answered and some were not. I did not understand why, if God truly loved us, that we were allowed to suffer so much. And although I did not think of Him as the bearded fellow on the ceiling of the Sistine Chapel, I did not know how else to think of Him.

So, it was a revelation to hear an explanation of and introduction to God that was so detailed, complete, and utterly benevolent. God is a living being, a soul, a finite point of light, who is the embodiment of all virtues. It is only due to the limitations of the English language that we use masculine pronouns to refer to God, but He is both our spiritual mother and father. And, as our parent, He wants the best for us. He does not want us to suffer.

But His role is not to wave a magic wand and make right every wrong. It is we who must transform ourselves in order to transform the world. If He fixed everything, from where would our self-respect come? From where would our love for the self come? How would we learn to take responsibility for ourselves, for our actions, if God fixed everything we broke? But knowing this, we know we cannot do it on our own. We need God's power to help us help ourselves.

Although I never really had an issue with God, as I did not feel He was to blame for our suffering, I did, however, have an issue with the state of the world, where life seemed unfair and unjust. So, for me to return to happiness, I needed to understand why things happened.

"God loves us the way we are, but too much to leave us that way."
Leighton Ford

# Why Do Things Happen?

"So why do things happen? How does life work?
Tell me the truth, so I will no longer hurt."

"It's really quite simple. One thing you must know.
Always remember: you reap what you sow."

I had heard this before and it didn't make sense.
If I thought about it much, it made me quite tense.

It was the law of karma, of choice and consequence,
Some say cause and effect, but to me it was nonsense.

So I said, "It can't be true. And I can prove that it's not.
When a child suffers, it couldn't have sown what it got."

"You're looking at the body and not at the soul.
The body may be young, but the soul may be old.

It is the soul that reaps and the soul that sows.
*This* is the secret everyone must know.

A soul carries with it from birth to birth
How it's treated everything on this great earth.

So it's like a magnet that repels and attracts,
From situations to people, the soul adds and subtracts."

"I've heard this before, you can attract what you desire."
She laughed and said, "No, you attract what you require.

Please listen closely while I explain what I mean.
What is really happening is beyond what is seen.

A soul carries with it several kinds of accounts.
There is credit and debit of various amounts.

If you do something good, an account receives a credit.
If you do something bad, an account receives a debit.

The good and the bad can be thoughts, words, or deeds.
These impact your accounts, so be sure to take heed.

If you have a surplus, then things are going well.
If you have an overdraft, you'll be able to tell.

You may become ill. You may lose your money.
Your relationships may struggle and nothing will be funny.

This doesn't happen by accident. There are no mistakes.
Nothing happens by chance. It's a choice you have made.

It's your soul that has chosen who's your next of kin,
The looks that you have and the color of your skin,

Whether you're born into comfort or struggle for wealth,
Whether you are ill or in very good health.

Everything happens as the consequence of a choice.
If you can learn this, you will surely rejoice."

I could see the wisdom in what she had said.
But then another thought came into my head.

"But what about justice? I don't think I understand.
Some do awful things and just get a slap on the hand."

"Please understand from the wisdom you've received.
There is no injustice. Do not be deceived.

Justice always comes, but at its own pace.
And it may come when the soul wears a new face.

But this you can't see. So you don't think this way.
You judge and condemn, based solely on today.

You don't think of the future or know of the past,
You judge in the present and become mad so fast.

But what looks so wrong may actually be right.
The history between two souls is out of your sight.

Just realize this: everything will work out.
A better day is coming. Please have no doubt."

For some people, just hearing the word "karma" can make them
lose their happiness. This is because the term has been so misun-
derstood and misused that it sounds quite cruel.

Years ago, I accepted the law of karma as it applied to me, but
I rejected applying it to others. I did this because I thought I was
a good person and things were going well for me so I could say
I was reaping what I had sown. But I could not apply the law of
karma to others, as I could not explain why bad things happened
to good people. And certainly, if something tragic or traumatic
had happened to me or a loved one, I would have quickly tossed

the concept aside or written off the event, thinking the universe had simply made a terrible mistake. But now I understand the law of karma in such a way that it alleviates suffering, rather than heightens it.

The Hindi word "karma," if literally translated, means "my doings," although it is often translated to mean "destiny" or "fate," which is not accurate. These terms imply nothing can be done about what is happening and so there is a sense of resignation in them.

For instance, people may say it is their karma to be mistreated by someone, but in truth, it *was* their karma to *have been* treated terribly yesterday, but it is their responsibility to love and respect the self so much today that they do not allow anyone to mistreat them again. Therefore, karma is used to help accept what has happened in the past, but also be a guide for making choices in the present to improve the future.

To understand karma, we must realize the past is often longer than just one lifetime. Karma – and all laws of attraction for that matter – must be explained in the context of reincarnation or else it does not make sense and can become quite cruel. Unless we understand that everything the soul does is carried with it, from lifetime to lifetime, we cannot come to terms with why a small child suffers in a hospital or why a drug dealer lives in the lap of luxury. Both are aspects of credit and debit the soul has carried with it.

I initially resisted the law of karma for a few reasons. One reason was the application of it often seemed cold, uncaring, and mean-spirited. My teacher has said this is because people want to punish others, to make them pay for what they have done. This is often the subtext of the phrases: "She had it coming," "He got what he deserved," or "It serves her right." All of these phrases reflect the wisdom of karma, but also contain the desire for revenge, so this is not a benevolent way to use the law of karma. According to my teacher, when we want revenge and want people to suffer for what they have done, it kills the love within us and takes away our happiness.

Another reason I resisted the law of karma was because I was not sure about rebirth, which is critical to understanding why things happen.


*"I believe that we are solely responsible for our choices, and we have to accept the consequences of every deed, word and thought throughout our lifetime."*

Elizabeth Kubler-Ross

# Is There Rebirth?
# Or Do We Live Once and Leave?

"I hear what you're saying, but what do I believe?
Is there rebirth? Or do we live once and leave?

It's a strange idea, if not taught since birth
That we live many times on this great spinning earth.

I am open to the idea, but I need a bit of proof."
"That's okay," she said, "Just look at these youths."

Right before my eyes, she showed me a scene
Of souls whose memories hadn't been quite cleaned.

"Their memory from before has slipped through the cracks,
They will prove to you, their souls have come back."

There were very young children, who had incredible skill,
And performed far beyond what was within their will.

There were many others who since their early years
Had intense and seemingly irrational fears.

The angel explained the fear came from before.
An experience they'd had, which they'd deplored.

"It's stuck in their memory, but they don't understand.
The same thing happens, when you shake another's hand.

Have you ever had an instant attraction?
The body you don't know, but the soul stirs a reaction.

The flip side, of course, also happens, too:
An unexplainable repulsion of someone brand new.

It doesn't happen by chance. Your souls have a history.
You've known each other before. It is no great mystery."

I still wasn't sure. I didn't know what to think.
She said, "Watch this," and told me not to blink.

It was a documentary about a young lad.
Who could remember being both a husband and dad.

He knew all of the streets in his former town,
But couldn't explain the mark on his crown.

He found his old house and his previous wife.
And shared some secrets they'd had in their life.

But it was she who told him about the mark on his head.
It was in the same place where he'd been shot dead.

The trauma had left a mark on his soul,
That he'd taken with him to play his next role.

I said, "That's enough. I will open my mind."
The angel smiled and said, "It will help you be kind.

But to fully understand 'you reap what you sow,'
Please realize this: you won't come back as a crow!

Man has used this threat as a method to control.
To get you to behave and do as you're told.

But this isn't right. It's a great big mistake.
Human souls are always human, for goodness sakes."

Although I was not sure about rebirth, I was open to it, but I know that some have strong feelings against it. For me the most compelling evidence for rebirth are accounts given by children of previous lifetimes. In the film, *Life, Death, and Rebirth: The Story of Reincarnation*, there were numerous accounts of past lives given by small children, and upon investigation the details were indeed verified.

One such account was given by a young girl who claimed she had been a boy who had been hit and killed by a train. She said that she – as a little boy – had had two little sisters and the name of her father had been Thomas Benson. The little girl also identified the remains of the home she claimed to have lived in as a little boy. Out of curiosity, her mother checked the church registry and found that in 1875 a Thomas Benson, who worked on the railway, had two surviving daughters, and lived in the home identified by her daughter.

Other evidence to support reincarnation comes through past life regressions. In some regressions people begin speaking languages they have never studied and use words that have become obsolete. Others have described buildings in great detail in countries they have not visited in their current life and have been able to unearth artifacts that were buried or hidden centuries before.

Interestingly, some great philosophers believed in reincarnation. Socrates said, "I am confident that there truly is such a thing as living again, that the living spring from the dead, and that the souls of the dead are in existence." And Voltaire said, "It is not more surprising to be born twice than once; everything in nature is resurrection."

In spite of the evidence for rebirth, I simply embraced it because it was essential to understand why things happen. For me, looking at the world with all of the pain and suffering, I could not fully regain my happiness if I did not embrace some benevolent understanding about what was happening. In the absence of this understanding, I suffered and was bound to continue suffering.

With this said, when I first presented this poem I was asked what we are supposed to think if we do not believe in rebirth, but still want to be happy. To this, I would recommend doing some research and seeing where it leads. There are plenty of books that provide evidence of rebirth – or at least enough evidence to indicate that it is something worth considering. If, in the end, you still cannot accept rebirth, then consider thinking in the following two ways:

1. Embrace the concept of heaven and hell, so that there can be some form of "you reap what you sow" in the afterlife. So, if you live a good life, not causing pain or suffering for yourself or others, you go to heaven. And, if you use your life for ill, spreading pain and sorrow, you go to hell.
2. Accept that the world is an unjust place filled with pain and suffering.

I know people who do not like the concept of rebirth, but rather prefer the traditional belief of heaven and hell. But for me, that is far worse. I do not like the idea of even the most depraved killer being eternally damned to suffer. I much prefer to believe every soul will have a chance – at least a chance – to right the wrongs committed. I do not like the thought that a soul will have to endure the consequences of what has been done, but I accept this and it enables me to have mercy on everyone.

Understanding and accepting rebirth and karma also makes

me act responsibly, as I no longer think I can get away with anything. I know that somehow, in some way, all I do will come back to me. So, I make sure that I treat myself, others, and the planet with love and respect. To me, this is the most important aspect of karma, which is how to use the wisdom.

*"Reincarnation contains a most comforting explanation of reality by means of which Indian thought surmounts difficulties which baffle the thinkers of Europe."*
Albert Schweitzer

# How Do I Use the Law of Karma?

"So then, the law of karma, how do I use it?
Tell me the way so I will not misuse it."

"With a little wisdom, you will clearly see,
There is benefit in everything, even the sting of a bee.

You have some account to settle, some outstanding debt.
You have to pay it off. You just haven't done it yet."

"But what if you've sown seeds that reaped bitter fruit?"
"Be kind to yourself, but know your choice was at the root.

But whatever you did, you did without knowing
That thoughts, words, and deeds were actually sowing.

So now take responsibility for what has come.
Learn what you must and put to rest what you've done.

No matter what happens to someone else or to you,
Remember to see it with this wise point of view.

You reap what you sow. The soul plants the seeds.
The fruit that is reaped depends on the soul's deeds.

But do not ever think, 'She got what she deserved.'
This is negativity and to you it will be served.

## Chapter 10

Just use this wisdom to maintain your stage,
To check your intentions, and be wise like a sage.

Do not become upset when something transpires.
Settlement will occur, this is required.

So have love and mercy for those who sow bad seeds
They will one day experience the fruit of those bad deeds."

"And if I think ill of them, then I, too, am doing wrong."
The angel laughed, "Now we're singing the same song.

So always remember and don't ever forget:
You reap what you sow and you've sown what you get.

Every cause has an effect and every effect has a cause,
So be sure to choose wisely and take heed of this law.

Be free from violence in your thoughts, words, and deeds.
This applies to everything – even how you feed!

So please don't seek revenge or toy with tit for tat.
Just do whatever you'd wish to come back.

The secret of this wisdom keeps the mind at peace,
And allows the heart to love everyone with ease."

I couldn't help but laugh. It was such a big relief.
How many tears I had shed from all my false beliefs!

Could it be true there is rhyme and reason?
That justice will come in the right season?

If you reap what you sow, then you must sow good seeds.
Your mind must be fertile and free from old weeds.

Knowing all I had heard, everything made sense.
I was meant to be happy from this moment hence.

My resistance to the law of karma left me when I asked myself,
"What if it is not true? What if all of the accounts supporting
rebirth are just an elaborate ruse? Or, what if we are reborn, but
there is no rhyme or reason to it; we are just randomly born into
different circumstances? So, the world is still an unfair place
filled with pain and suffering. And yet, here I am, walking
around believing you reap what you sow. Then what?"

The answer was so clear, "There is no harm done." Why?
Because the law of karma – if used benevolently – helps and does
not harm in every aspect of time.

*Past* – For the past, karma helps me move into acceptance.
Whatever has happened, I need to take responsibility for it, as
somehow, in some way, I sowed those seeds. I cannot hang onto
anything or blame others for how they treated me. If there is
some lesson for me to learn, I must learn it and then let go, as the
past cannot be changed. This restores my self-respect and keeps
my mind at peace.

*Present* – In the present, karma helps keep me from feeling
sorrow about what is happening now. I used to suffer whenever
I heard a sad story about someone suffering somewhere. With
the understanding of karma, however, I realize all souls are
settling their accounts and it does not help others to suffer with
them. It also means I can have mercy on those who sow negative
seeds, as I know whatever people do will come back to them.
This keeps my heart loving, rather than swinging between
sorrow and anger.

*Future* – For the future, karma helps me check my actions now
to make sure I do everything with a good intention. I do not

want to sow any more bad seeds, because I know they will bring bitter fruit. Therefore, I need to learn to treat myself and others with love and respect, as that is what I would like to come back to me!

If we want to be happy, the application of karma ought to be benevolent and not used to judge or condemn. We also must not think that the bad things that happen are a form of punishment. We need to think that everything happens to either teach us something new or to settle an account. When we learn something new, it is good. After we settle an account, just like paying off a debt, we feel light because we have paid off that debt and we will not have to pay it off again.

With this said, I can understand that those who have faced difficulties in life may still find the law of karma a bitter pill to swallow. What is heartening to me is that I have watched my teacher, who has been thoroughly tested by life in almost every way, use her understanding of karma to help her maintain her happiness no matter what she faces. Aside from running a meditation center and tirelessly serving the community, she supports her husband with his dementia and her son with his learning disability. To this day, she deals with challenges very few would be able to cope with without suffering, and yet she manages to do so.

For me, understanding karma was the last piece of wisdom that helped restore my peace of mind. This is not to say my mind is always peaceful. Sometimes I am still affected by something that has happened. But when I notice my mind is not at peace, I know it is an unnatural and unhealthy state and I need to sit down and figure out why. In any event, it means I have moved away from wisdom, from truth, and I need to pull myself back.

Most of the time, when my mind is not at peace, I have forgotten who I am – a soul – and am thinking I am a body. I am thinking in terms of *I* and *my*. In this state, I feel hurt, insult, fear, or worry. I am affected by what others say and do and what happens to them, as I am not sustaining myself, but am looking for others to sustain me. I have forgotten that everything will work out and a better day is coming. And, I am not connected to God, but rather trying to take whatever love, respect, and appreciation I can extract from those closest to me – whether they are friends, family members, or even strangers.

When I realize what is happening and correct it, my mind becomes peaceful again. There is no better feeling than bringing peace into a mind that was stirring with turmoil. When I am able to do this, I feel a sense of achievement. And then the little spark of love I had for myself burns a little brighter, because I have improved the quality of my thoughts and therefore my life.

In this state, I want more than just peace of mind. I want love, too. So this becomes the practice, to keep my mind at peace and to bring love back into my heart.

*"How people treat you is their karma; how you react is yours."*
Wayne Dyer

# PART TWO

## The Practice of Happiness:

## Returning Love to the Heart

# How Can I Create Happiness?

To never again ask, "Why?" I made a solemn vow.
And turned my attention to the question of how.

"So how can I create happiness? What must I do?
What is the secret? Tell me your view."

"First you must know what happiness is.
Without this wisdom, you cannot pass the quiz.

As I said in the beginning, it occurs at a time
When there's love in the heart and peace in the mind.

It's important to remember what you've been told.
Your head and your heart are under *your* control.

So no one and nothing can make you feel sad
Without your consent, you cannot feel bad.

Happiness doesn't depend on something out there.
You create it on the inside, although this is rare.

But this is a skill that's essential for life.
Otherwise many things can cut like a knife.

The good news is this skill can be learned,
With practice and patience at every turn.

But you also must know what it is not.
Pleasure isn't happiness, though you seek this a lot.

Pleasure is something derived from a sense.
You feel a quick buzz, but then crave it hence.

The senses will make you always want more.
Then receiving what you want, becomes your only chore.

But whenever you're wanting, your mind cannot rest,
Your heart will ache, and you won't feel the best.

In the shadow of pleasure is an unspoken fear,
You won't receive what you need, then there'll be tears.

Your happiness is lost when you pursue pleasure,
Even the subtle ones that cannot be measured,

Like love, respect, appreciation, and regard.
When you don't receive these, you fall down so hard.

Pleasure will surely cause you to suffer.
Wanting from the outside makes life so much tougher.

So don't use your body to seek every pleasure.
A soul deserves happiness, life's only treasure."

I used to think that pursuing pleasure meant chasing after the obvious physical indulgences, like food, drink, cigarettes, or sex. But I did not know that pursuing pleasure can be as subtle as wanting to see a smile on my daughter's face when I walk in the door. And while I do not suffer from any physical addictions, I was surprised to discover that I was not free from the subtle spiritual addictions of wanting to be accepted and feeling a sense of security and belonging.

While loved ones often intervene when someone is suffering from a physical addiction, no one usually intervenes when we suffer from spiritual addictions. This is probably because very few people are free from spiritual addictions. So we tend to think that spiritual addictions are normal. It is alright to want to be greeted with a smile when we walk in the door; there is no harm in it.

And certainly, as long as we do not base our happiness on whether we get a smile or not, it is fine. But what is the state of our happiness when we do not get what we want? What lengths do we go to in order to get what we want? What loss is created for the self and others when we pursue the subtle spiritual pleasures?

The problem is that sometimes we get what we are looking for, whether it is appreciation, approval, or regard, and we register that as happiness. It makes us feel a little better about ourselves and so we start working to receive more and more of what we require. Soon we may find ourselves working, exercising or volunteering to excess in the pursuit of receiving something from outside of ourselves. Unfortunately, this kind of happiness is temporary and it traps us in having to receive from others.

And we know that when we do not receive what we want, we lose our happiness. So we live in fear of whether or not we will receive what we need. When our sense of worth comes from the outside, our happiness is not our own. Then we open ourselves up to suffering every time things do not happen as we wish.

What invariably happens when we pursue pleasure is we start to try to control everything and everyone so things will happen in a way that will maintain our happiness. I see this in my interactions with my daughter. I know there are two types of corrections I give her. One type is to uplift her, to share something with her that she needs to know to be content or kind.

The other type is when I am trying to control her; I want her to stop doing whatever she is doing that is pressing my buttons and taking away my happiness. This is apparent when we do something messy together. When we cook, my voice is strained with tension as I say, "Try to keep the flour in the bowl," as cumulous clouds form in our kitchen. The irony is that she is actually very careful and tidy. Whether she was this way naturally or has become this way after being micro-managed, I do not know.

But now I make an effort to remember a few things whenever we do something messy together. First, we are supposed to be having fun. And we will both have a lot more fun if I remember that almost everything can be fixed, cleaned, repainted, or replaced. Second, she is supposed to be exploring our world and improving her coordination, so I need to allow her to do so. And third, and most importantly, we do these activities so she can teach me how to be more patient, tolerant and certainly less controlling.

I have realized that success in controlling her – and others for that matter – is temporary. I may win the battle when she stops doing something so I can be peaceful again, but I have lost the war. My happiness still depends on what she does, so I am still dependent on her to do what I need her to do. In effect, she is the master and I am the servant. She is in charge of my state of being. And worse yet, by trying to control her, I am teaching her to be subservient, that she must do as I say. I may think this is acceptable, because I will not abuse this power over her. But in truth, I am not helping her live up to her potential and I know someone who is controlled by one will easily be controlled by another.

Interestingly, I have read that adult children often make drastic life changes after their parents die. When they no longer feel that they have to please someone, they feel free to do what they want. So, they change careers, divorce spouses, and move to new places. This is another loss associated with pursuing pleasure. When we live to please someone else, we are not always pleased with the self.

I do not want this to happen with my daughter. So, I am learning to deal with and control what happens inside of me, so I will not try to control what happens outside of me. When I can do this, I will become the master of myself and the servant of no one. Then, the only corrections I will give my daughter will be to uplift and we will both be better for it.

In truth, happiness is generated within. We are not used to doing this, so it seems harder to pursue happiness than pleasure. But actually, it is easier when you realize you can create happiness without trying to control everyone and everything, which is actually the hardest thing we do each day. I want to reach the state where I am in control of myself no matter what is happening around me. When I am sitting in class, listening to my teacher describe this internal state, I know this is what I want for myself. The question is: "How?"

*"The superior man thinks always of virtue; the common man thinks of comfort."*
Confucius

# H - Have the "Right" Thoughts

"So, where is this treasure? Please give me the map.
How do I find it and hold it in my lap?"

"Keep peace in your mind, as I said at the start.
When the mind is at peace, then love fills your heart.

Peace makes you stable and love makes you secure.
Then happiness is yours. This will surely occur.

If you think the 'right' way, then you'll feel the 'right' way.
When you learn to do this, it's the most wonderful day.

The mind becomes quiet and all thinking ceases.
Your heart feels love and heals the broken pieces.

The incredible irony is to be free from all thought
You must begin by thinking rather than by not!

When the soul is weak, negative thoughts are the norm.
It is this way of thinking that causes mental storms.

If you want to be happy, you must strengthen the soul,
You must think in a new way and let go of the old.

Every time a negative thought comes into your mind,
You must replace it with another, something that is kind.

Make use of the wisdom you have just learned
To make sense of situations and keep from getting burned.

You have to use your mind in a beneficial manner
And no longer entertain negative internal banter."

I was quiet for a moment, digesting what she said.
And then a negative thought came into my head.

I wasn't quite sure, if I should share what I'd thought.
It may seem as if I hadn't learned what she'd taught.

But she had told me to ask. This was her suggestion.
This was my chance. I had to ask every question.

So I said, "'Think positively,' is what I heard you say.
Forgive me for saying so, but isn't that a cliché?"

"Others say, 'Think positively.' This I do not doubt.
But *I* give you something positive of which to think about.

I have told you about God, that you are a soul,
Everything will work out, and happiness is your goal.

I have told you why things happen, that nothing is unfair.
Now I'll tell you this, since you've asked me to share.

Positive thoughts are good, but the 'right' thoughts you need.
Thoughts based on wisdom, these thoughts are the seed.

The fruit of these thoughts is love in the heart.
Then happiness will come. So 'right' thoughts are the start."

My teacher often says the quality of our thoughts determines the quality of our life. If we consider the average person has around 70,000 thoughts a day, we have to ask ourselves, "What kind of a life am I creating with the thoughts I am having? What is the quality of my thoughts about myself, others, work, life, money, health, relationships, and the past, not to mention the future? And how do these thoughts make me feel? Do they perk me up or bring me down?"

I did not think much about my thoughts until I came to The Spiritual University. I just thought my mind, like everyone else's mind, constantly produced thoughts. I did not think much about the effect those thoughts had on myself or others. And I certainly did not think I could have much of an influence over my thoughts. My mind simply produced thoughts and those thoughts made me feel good, bad, or indifferent.

Because our thoughts are so crucial to our state of being, the first course I took at The Spiritual University was the Positive Thinking Course. Although many things were covered, I only retained and used one thing from the entire course. But that one thing was such a gem that it continues to improve the quality of my life. And what was that one thing? The wisdom of recognizing and disposing of waste thoughts.

What is a waste thought? It is just that. A waste. A waste of time and energy. It is a thought that is of no benefit. It is usually about something outside of our control, whether it is about the past, or someone else's behavior or opinion, or thoughts about an imagined future. No matter how long and hard we consider a waste thought, nothing good can arise from it, as there is nothing we can do about it. It simply drains our energy.

As soon as I heard this, I shared this gem with my husband. He, too, immediately saw the wisdom in it, and then we began checking our own thoughts, but also each other's. When either one of us would say something like, "If only we had done *this* and not *that*," or, "I wonder what so-and-so thought of my presentation," then the other one would declare, "Waste thought!" While I would not do this with anyone else, since my husband and I were on the same page as far as waste thoughts were concerned, it was a good way to catch ourselves when we were falling back into old patterns of thinking.

Doing this also made me realize I could have an influence, if even a little bit, over what thoughts I allowed my mind to entertain. I found I could, at least sometimes, redirect my thoughts away from a waste thought. The added benefit of this is that waste thoughts often degenerate into negative thoughts. So, if we can learn to throw away a waste thought early, then we will not have to struggle to free ourselves from a negative thought later, which is often more challenging.

We have all had the experience of our minds being consumed with some negative thought from which we cannot free ourselves. During these times, we feel as if there is nothing we can do to free ourselves from our thoughts. We are at the mercy of them. When we are in this state, my teacher often says, "Sit down, and give yourself understanding." We need to explore more deeply from where our thoughts are coming, so we can make a shift within. Once we realize what was at the root of our thoughts, we can replace a negative thought with a "right" thought.

A "right" thought is based on wisdom and is therefore positive or beneficial. It causes no harm to the self or others. In practice, we need to identify when our thoughts have turned against us and replace them with something positive or more beneficial.

For instance, when our happiness decreases, usually we have forgotten who we are and are thinking we are a body and not a soul. In this state, we look to take love, respect, appreciation, or regard from the outside and bring it inside.

So, we need to remember: *I am a soul. I already have everything I need. I am peace. I am love. I need not take anything from others because I am full. I do not require anything from anyone. And if I am lacking something, then let me give myself what I require.*

When our thoughts are pulled down by things happening to us or others, we need to remember: *Everything that happens is determined by our karma. At every moment, we are reaping the fruit of the seeds we have sown in the past. There is no reason to become influenced by what happens. Everything is accurate. It must happen to clear our karmic accounts. Everything passes and in the end, everything will be all right.*

When we are feeling fear over a loss, we need to realize that we are thinking we possess something, but this is an illusion. During these times, we need to remember: *A soul owns nothing and so it cannot lose anything. As a soul, I came into this world alone and I will leave on my own. I am a child of God and belong to Him alone. Everyone else is also a child of God and therefore my sibling. Let me have love for everyone, not just for a few.*

Often, when we have allowed what someone has said or done to hurt us, it is because we are thinking that others should sustain us by behaving in a certain way and yet they have not lived up to our expectations. At this time, we need to remember what Dadi Janki, the administrative head of The Spiritual University, often says: "It is the duty of other people to insult and defame you. It is your responsibility to not be affected by what they say."

The benefit of working with our thoughts is that over time it becomes more natural. Then one day we realize our perception has shifted and our attitude has changed. Whereas before we may have had a negative thought – or many negative thoughts – about someone's intention, now we give him or her the benefit of the doubt and do not waste another moment thinking about it. This helps keep our minds at peace and allow our hearts to love.

While positive thoughts are at the core of "right" thinking, positive thoughts that are not based on wisdom will not restore happiness for long. Without coming to a deeper understanding about who we are, why we are here, or why things happen, positive thoughts are merely hoping the bad things happening all around will not affect us or our loved ones. How long can this be maintained?

What we must realize through "right" thinking is that there is benefit in everything. Even though we may not be able to see it at the time, we must have the faith and wisdom to know that there will be some benefit. The following parable illustrates this:

*A king and his most trusted advisor were hunting together in a forest with some of the king's soldiers. When the king was cutting an apple to eat, he accidentally cut off the tip of his finger. As he bandaged the wound, he turned to his advisor and asked why such a terrible thing had happened to him.*

*The advisor told the king it was not terrible and that there was benefit in everything. The king was so angered by the advisor's remark he ordered his soldiers to take the advisor back to the castle and throw him in the dungeon.*

*An hour later, as the king wandered the forest alone, he was captured by a tribe. As the tribe prepared the king for a sacrifice, the high priest noticed the wound on the king's finger. Seeing the king would be an imperfect offering to their gods, the high priest ordered the king to be released.*

*The king rushed back to his castle and went straight to the dungeon to free his advisor. As soon as he saw the advisor, he told him what happened and apologized for sending him to the dungeon. He admitted he did not know it at the time, but there was benefit in what had happened to his finger.*

*The advisor agreed and said, "For me, too, there was benefit. If you had not sent me to the dungeon, I would have been the one sacrificed."*

President Nelson Mandela is an inspiring example of looking for the benefit in something. I remember seeing an interview with him when he was asked why he was not bitter about spending 27 years of his life in prison. He replied with a gentle laugh and said, "In a way, it was good. It gave me a chance to think." If only we could all use our thoughts in such a way that no matter what we faced we tried to find some benefit in it.

"Right" thinking is about using the estimated 70,000 thoughts we have each day to improve the quality of our life. It means replacing the negative waste thoughts that often fill our minds, with positive empowering thoughts about what we are meant to be thinking, feeling, and doing. We do not realize the power of our thoughts, how our thoughts determine how we feel and, more subtly, how they radiate from us and have an effect on those around us. But retraining the mind to think in a new way takes practice, which begins by increasing awareness of the self.

*"The problems that we have today cannot be solved with the same level of thinking that created them."*
Albert Einstein

13

# A - Awareness of the Self

"I will try to keep the 'right' thoughts in my mind,
To keep them on wisdom and make sure they are kind."

"To think the 'right' thoughts, awareness is the key.
You have to ask yourself, 'What's happening in me?'

What am I thinking? What am I feeling?'
Keep your awareness on this if you want to begin healing.

It won't take long to see what's happening inside.
The mind is undisciplined; it's on a wild ride.

It travels to the past, wallowing in what has been done,
Then jumps to the future, worrying what is to come.

It leaps from person to person, thinking what others must do.
It spins with old thoughts, rarely thinking something new.

And how does the heart feel? Have this you realized?
It's aching and empty. This should be no surprise.

With all of this spinning, the heart can't create love.
So it looks to other people, forgetting to look up above.

It either chases after others hoping it will receive,
Or runs the other way when it doesn't get what it needs.

Then it cares for just a few and is quick to make you cry.
The heart has shut down; it's so brittle and dry.

It's time to become aware of what's happening inside,
If you are to make a change and get on a different ride.

Once you become aware, a realization must come next.
Find out what's at the root, why you're sad or vexed.

Have you forgotten who you are? Or want others to provide?
Which one of the vices is stirring you up inside?

Have you forgotten about karma? Or thinking life's unfair?
Are you blaming others? Or making the mistake to compare?

So take responsibility, don't blame others for your state.
Everything is happening to see what you'll create.

Will you try to take your happiness from outside?
Or will you learn to create it? To generate it inside?

This can only happen if you become aware,
Realize your mistake, and then do something rare.

You must transform yourself, turn lead into gold,
Take responsibility, and strengthen your soul.

Use every moment to restore your peace of mind
And bring love in your heart, to last you throughout time."

Before I started studying at The Spiritual University – and I regret to admit for a long time after – I was very aware of what everyone else needed to do. I could spot everyone else's faults, defects, and shortcomings, whether of a close relation or a distant president, but not my own.

For instance, when I was in class and my teacher would say, "Someone in a state of ego will not be able to say, 'Sorry' or 'Thank you.'" I would immediately think of a time someone broke something in my house and did not say, "Sorry." I would not see the ego in me recalling that incident or search my memory for the times I did not say "Sorry" or "Thank you."

I continued like this for quite a while, attending class and enjoying the revelations I had about others' weaknesses, but not my own. This was, of course, because I still believed myself to be perfect! But then the day came – and I cannot even give a reason for how or why the shift came – when I began to see my own weaknesses.

And then, it was not so enjoyable to attend class anymore! I felt turmoil when I saw so much falsehood within, how there was such a discrepancy between the inside and the outside, how dependent I was on other people's approval and appreciation, and how much support I took from friends and family. I still never missed a class, even though it sometimes pained me to hear my teacher identify some weakness I felt was within me, because I knew that is where I had to be if I were to free myself.

Now I spend a lot less time thinking about the faults, defects, and shortcomings of others. And when I find myself thinking of others' defects, I ask myself why I am entertaining these thoughts when I have yet to free myself from my own weaknesses. Once I become perfect, truly perfect – where my happiness depends on no one and nothing, because I am the embodiment of all the virtues – then I can allow myself to think about what others do. But then, of course, when I am in that state, I will not be able to see others' defects, as you cannot see in others what you do not have within yourself.

When we decide we want to change the self, and not others,

we need to turn our attention inward and follow the path my teacher describes as an ART: Awareness, Realization, and Transformation. We need to become aware of what is happening inside. This means watching each reaction that occurs and seeing when we feel good or bad. If we stop with just awareness, we may become disheartened about all of the negativity within and give up. We must have realizations about the weakness we have identified, so we can transform the self. These are a few questions I ask myself to help bring a realization:

*What was I looking for that I did not receive?*
*What am I hanging onto that I need to let go of?*
*What was my intention?*
*Am I blaming someone else for my state of being?*
*Were my thoughts or words respectful of myself and others?*
*Was I being loving, inclusive, and generous?*
*Am I thinking negatively of others?*
*Am I wishing for people or situations to be different than they are?*
*What can I do in the face of what has been done?*

Realizations occur when we become aware of what was behind whatever we were thinking, feeling, saying, or doing. For instance, we realize we over-extended ourselves because we were looking for approval, appreciation, or acceptance. Or we became hurt or upset because someone did not give us the love or respect for which we were searching. Or we were disappointed in the self because we wanted to project a perfect image of the self and were not able to do so.

In the beginning, I would often waste time trying to have a realization about someone else, as to why he or she was acting a certain way. If we can quickly do this and come into a state of understanding or acceptance so we can let it go, then this is fine. But if too much time is spent, it can turn into a negative habit. For instance, if I saw someone acting disrespectfully, I would allow myself to think about that. But more can be gained by turning our attention to the self and asking if it is respectful to focus on someone else's defects or if *I* always respect others through my thoughts, words, and deeds.

The problem with dwelling on others' defects is that we taste the negativity of doing so. My teacher often says when we think negatively about someone "it is like drinking poison and hoping the other will die. When we think negatively, we feel negatively. Other people may be completely oblivious to what we are thinking, but we will feel anger or jealousy or whatever it is that we keep in our minds."

If we keep our awareness on ourselves, we will have realizations. And once we have a realization, we can make a shift within and transform the self. To be able to do this successfully requires great honesty. My teacher believes that honesty – with the self – is essential for happiness.

I feel I am fairly aware of what happens in my head and heart, and fairly good at realizing where I have gone wrong, but sometimes the transformation just does not occur. I still cannot free myself from some thought or feeling – usually about something I have said or done that I am now questioning. At these times, I need to sit down and try to figure out what is happening within. I find it helpful to write things down. Then I can usually see more clearly what is happening inside and make a shift.

If I am thinking about something I have said or done that has upset someone, I ask myself if I have done something wrong. If I have and it is possible to remedy it, I do that. But if I have not done anything wrong, then often I see that I am trying to make sure everyone's happy with me so I can be happy with myself. I realize I have to let go of this habit of basing my happiness on how others feel about me. I am falling into the old trap of trying to take my happiness from others and not creating my happiness within.

To be able to increase our awareness and realizations, which enables transformation, we need to know "the enemy within."

*"If we had no faults of our own, we would not take so much pleasure in noticing those of others."*
François de la Rochefoucauld

# P – Possess Self-Respect, Not Ego

"So if I keep awareness, what should be the effect?"
"To let go of your ego and possess self-respect.

Remember what I told you, about when the soul was full.
It could sustain the self; it wasn't pushed or pulled.

But then it lost energy and became so very weak.
Then the ego came into you and said you must seek.

It whispered in your ear that your happiness is outside.
You believed this falsehood, not knowing that it lied."

I had heard about the ego when I studied back in school.
But I couldn't remember much and felt a bit of a fool.

I told the angel this and then asked what the ego was.
I also wanted to know what exactly the ego does.

"The ego occupies the head and keeps your thoughts reeling.
This assaults the heart and keeps it from feeling.

It is so very possessive. It always thinks *I* or *mine*.
You can tell when it's active. There are so many signs.

The moment you feel insulted, know the ego is to blame.
It causes you to react and engage in hurtful games."

The angel went on and on, describing how the ego manifests.
It was such a long list. I began to feel depressed!

"So how can I be positive, knowing the ego is within me?
It seems I have no chance. There's too much negativity."

"Before you lived in darkness, not knowing there was light.
You thought negativity was normal and didn't put up a fight.

But the ego isn't you. It isn't who you are.
You're the embodiment of goodness, the light of a star.

So now the ego must go. It cannot stay within you."
"But how can I dispose of it? What must I do?"

"You must starve it of nourishment. You cannot let it feed.
You must do what it can't bear and not give it what it needs.

Since the ego loves resistance, you must be quick to accept.
This doesn't mean agreeing, it just means you don't reject.

You must accept situations and people as they are.
If you can do this, I promise you'll go far.

The ego will always recall everything that has passed.
It keeps you from the present, this is its favorite task.

It reminds you of the bad someone else has done,
To prop yourself up and make you think you've won.

So let go of the past, bring your thoughts to the present.
Don't think about others. This makes the heart feel pleasant.

The ego makes you want to change everyone.
You must know this battle is one that can't be won.

The battle is within. This one must be fought.
It isn't done with weapons, but with the power of thought.

Watch every thought; replace the bad with the good.
Be aware of your reactions and then do what you should.

You came to this earth to heal all that's broken.
So be careful of your thoughts and each word that is spoken.

This means letting go of ego and possessing self-respect.
Then your heart will open. It's a guaranteed effect."

Years ago, if you had asked me if there were a connection between self-respect and happiness, I would have said self-respect was essential for happiness. But in my mind, self-respect was linked to receiving respect from others. And certainly, I had respect for myself as long as others had respect for me. But when others did not give me the respect I sought, the respect I had for myself declined and my happiness fell along with it.

In this, I know I am not alone. We have all had occasions when someone did not give us respect and then we lost our happiness. This struggle to receive respect from others is a constant theme in life. There are countless stories in the news about someone who sought respect from another, but sadly, the quest ended tragically.

At one point, I know I identified with my profession and the respect I had for myself was tied to it. I moved to Japan when I was 23 and worked for a leading businessman in a large Japanese company. Upon reflection, I realize I had a mini-celebrity status in the company, as I was an assistant to the chairman and was one of only a handful of foreigners in the company. This boosted my sense of who I was and made me feel special. And because of this, even after I left Japan, I would often tell stories of what I had experienced there in an attempt to gain others' respect.

As I have begun to understand more about ego and self-respect, I am beginning to think I had respect for myself because of what I had achieved, but not necessarily for who I was on the inside. But true self-respect is not derived from what we have accomplished. It is evident in how we do what we do. It is not tied to a result, or an outcome, or a temporary status that is here one day and gone the next. It occurs when we realize we do not need to be seen as special or as a celebrity, because in God's eyes, we are all celebrities, we are all special. And who else's opinion really matters?

Now if I were to reflect on my experience in Japan, I would look for the qualities in me that made the experience possible. As I moved there without a job, I can see I had both courage and faith. I had the courage to step into the unknown and faith in myself to know it would turn out well. In adjusting to life there, I can see I was flexible and open. I reserved judgment and accepted things as they were.

As for recognizing my need for others to see me as special or different, I now know that this arises when there is a lack of love for the self. When we lack love, we look for others to tell us we are good because we are not so sure we are. In this state, we do not have self-respect, as we are dependent on others to give us love and respect so we can feel good about ourselves. When we recognize this within, we need to restore our self-respect and let go of our egos, which takes away our happiness.

Signs of ego include:
**Identifying with the body** and thinking in terms of *I* and *my*. For example, *I* am a certain nationality, gender, race, religion; *I* am a spouse, parent, sibling, in-law, employee or employer; and

these are *my* ideas, beliefs, family members, and friends.

**Getting caught up in the "R's"** of reacting, recalling, resisting, rejecting, or seeking revenge. Seeking revenge can be as subtle as trying to teach someone a lesson, pointing out where someone has made a mistake, or giving the silent treatment.

**Engaging in the "C's"** of comparing, competing, criticizing, or condemning. All of these keep the heart from experiencing love.

**Thinking, "I am right."** This includes judging someone as bad or not as good as we think he or she should be, thinking negatively about what someone has said or done, and repeating someone's low point to another.

To restore self-respect, we need to:
**Remember who we are.** I am a soul who is worthy, eternal, and special. Realize no two souls are alike; we are unique and already have everything we need.

**Recognize we have an important role to play**. God needs us and cannot do His work on earth without us lending Him the purity of our minds, thoughts, words, and actions.

**Take responsibility** for our state of being and blame no one for it. We need to accept that our thoughts create our feelings and that our karma has drawn certain people and experiences to us, so no one else is to blame for our happiness or sadness.

**Focus on strengths** and have the highest vision of the self and others. While we may think that we have, or someone else has, ninety-nine negative qualities, we must find and focus on the one good quality within us and others.

**Shift within** to stop our suffering by thinking, speaking, and acting in a new way. When we change our state of being through our effort, we feel a sense of accomplishment and goodness within.

On the path to happiness, my teacher will never talk about the need to *receive* respect to be happy. In fact, she says receiving respect traps us and makes us dependent on others. It is much better when others disrespect, insult, or defame us, as this creates fertile ground to learn how to regain our happiness. Why? Because it is only when our egos have been wounded that we begin to do the inner work we need to do to restore our self-respect.

And interestingly, while my teacher does not mention the need to *receive* respect to restore our happiness, she does talk about the need to *give* respect to recover our self-respect. Now I keep my awareness on this. How am I thinking and speaking about others? How am I speaking to others? Do I always give others respect? Or, do I give respect selectively, only after I receive it?

When we develop true self-respect, it emerges from within and is constant. It does not fluctuate based on the words or behavior of others. It does not rise with praise or fall with defamation. It is not bestowed on us by others and therefore it cannot be taken away from us. It is something we generate within, and therefore it is not dependent on the outside world.

I now know self-respect is essential for happiness. But it does not occur after *receiving* respect; it arises after *giving* it. Only when we can give respect, to all people at all times in all circumstances, can our minds become peaceful and our hearts become loving. Therefore, our happiness depends on restoring our self-respect. Without it, we cannot begin to know what love is.

*"They cannot take away our self-respect if we do not give it to them."*

Mahatma Gandhi

# P - Prefer No One, Love All

"In self-respect, you won't prefer one over another.
You will love all, with the warmth of a mother.

Know the ego loves opinions and to separate and divide.
But if you were truly wise, you would never pick a side.

No matter what you heard, you don't know the whole story.
You don't know the past or if the future will bring glory.

So when two are posed to battle or engage in a terrible war,
Why not send good wishes to both and not pollute your core?

Or else what will happen? You'll root for one over another.
But the one you root against is God's child and your brother.

Will you cheer his defeat? Will you relish his downfall?
Will this bring peace of mind and make you feel love for all?

A preference for one means a prejudice against another.
This keeps the heart closed, from loving all like a mother."

I wanted to know more, to know what true love was.
I asked her to explain, to tell me what love does.

The angel replied, "Love. This word's been so misused.
If you don't know what it is, you can end up feeling abused.

But to begin to know what it is, you must know what it's not.
It's not remotely similar to what you have been taught.

The love you have today is tied to your physical form.
It's based on birth and marriage. This has become the norm.

It's a kind of a bargain you make just with a few.
You say, 'I will love you, if you promise to love me, too.'

This sounds like a good idea, since you both want to receive.
The problem with this is you can't give if you're in need.

Soon the time comes, when the promise is broken.
Then your heart breaks, when hurtful words are spoken.

The bargains you make have requirements and conditions.
Others must perform with absolute precision.

When they fail to do so, your loving feeling alters.
And then your faith in others soon begins to falter.

In truth there is no way this promise can be kept.
When someone you love dies, you'll feel you have been left.

So fear lurks in the shadow of this bargain you have made.
Your happiness depends on others, for long it may not stay.

And when there's fear you suffer, of this you can be sure.
There is no peace of mind, if your love's not pure."

This isn't what I wanted. It isn't how life should be.
But what was the alternative? I asked the angel to tell me.

"The love you must find cannot be of this earth.
It must be metaphysical and come from your self-worth.

It isn't to be found in the twinkle of an eye.
And it cannot be taken from someone who will die.

Love emerges from within. It's something you create.
It's not taken from others, but something you radiate.

When you're in this state, all others receive from you.
Not just those you know or a few you pick and choose.

In this state of fullness, all desires fade away.
You have all you need, each and every day.

Your fears will fall away, as this love makes you secure.
You'll no longer be so needy, when your love is pure."

When I started to see how preferences for some lead to prejudices against others, I began to see how tainted and tarnished my heart had become. Then I discovered that while we often prefer those with whom we identify, we are often hardest on them. Sure, sometimes we give them the greatest leeway, as is often the case with our children. But in the end, we want them to perform to their highest standard, as we see what they do as a reflection on us and we want to be seen in a positive light.

Two examples that illustrate this come to mind. The summer after September 11, 2001, a few Muslim laborers were painting the outside of our flat in London. As my desk was next to the balcony and they congregated there for meals, on one occasion we talked about that day. The one whose English was the strongest was so angry about what the hijackers had done. He asked me, "But don't you hate them? Don't you hate them for what they did to your country?"

I did not lose any friends or relatives that day, and I recognize that I may have responded differently if I had, but without hesitation I said, "I have nothing but mercy for those men. They lived their lives filled with anger and hatred, spending their days plotting to spread sorrow and suffering. What a horrific way to live." It was easy for me to have mercy for those men, because I did not identify with them. They were from another religion and other countries, and I did not feel their actions reflected on me. But for the painter, it was different. In his view, the hijackers had defamed him and his religion, and so he had no love for them.

But then, how did I feel when images of American soldiers acting inappropriately with prisoners of war were in the news? Or when high-level American officials were speaking or acting against what I thought to be just and right? Did I have love in my heart for them? Even a tiny bit of mercy? Not much. I felt quite right in judging and condemning them.

I now realize that although I was raised as a Catholic and worshipped Christ for his capacity to love, I never worked to become that loving myself. I did not remotely come close to the depth of love captured in Christ's words when he said, "Forgive them, Father, for they know not what they do." I was quite happy to divide the world into those whom I loved and those whom I did not. Essentially, I loved those who did as I liked and I did not love those who did otherwise, which is not exactly Christ-like.

My teacher says the first step toward becoming truly loving towards all is to let go of the false identities associated with the body and remember who we are. A soul has no religion, nationality, political affiliation, or family ties. The sooner we stop identifying ourselves in these ways, the sooner we can see others as souls, playing their roles here on earth. And better yet, we can learn to see each and every one of them as helping to push us towards perfection, where we can be loving towards all.

My teacher often shares a piece of wisdom her teacher shared with her when she started on this path: "If you have hatred, or even the slightest trace of dislike, for even one of God's children, you cannot experience God's love." This is how clean our hearts must be. This is how loving we must become. G. K. Chesterton said it well when he said, "Love means to love that which is unlovable; or it is no virtue at all."

Now, my teacher is also very practical. She knows if we have allowed someone to hurt us, it is very hard to be loving toward that person. So she recommends asking God to give love to that soul for you. I have done this and it is incredible how this one simple benevolent action opened my heart and made me feel loving again.

Learning to love all is not just about being in a state of forgiveness, it is about having good wishes for all, not just a few. Various people often tell my teacher they wish their spouse or child would be cured of some illness, hired for a certain position, or would reconcile with a loved one. To this my teacher sometimes says, "But what about the rest of humanity? Why have good wishes for just one or two or three people you know? Why not have good wishes for all?"

The truth is that we want good things to happen to our loved ones because it is from this that we derive our happiness. And by the same token, we feel sorrow when those with whom we are close suffer. So in truth, our hopes for a few are really desires for our own happiness.

I can see this in myself when I drop my daughter off at school or an extra-curricular activity. Sometimes I find myself thinking, "I hope she has a good time." This is fine, of course, provided my happiness does not depend on whether or not she does. But why not be unlimited and wish that all of the children, and teachers for that matter, enjoy their day? Why just my daughter?

But this is not how we live our lives. Our love is tied to our physical form, which makes it subject to fluctuation. This brings pain and suffering and so our love is lost in the fog of fear over our potential for loss. While we are always free to love, in truth we yearn to *be* loved. Just as with respect, we want to receive love much more than we want to give it.

When we say the words, "I love you," we often say it not for the other person to hear it, but so we can hear the response it brings in return. My teacher often says, "When we say, 'I love you,' we actually mean, 'I need you.' Human love has become a state of dependency, a state of neediness."

Spiritual love, however, is very different. It arises from within and is based on the love we have for the self and God. It occurs from knowing who we are and recognizing our innate goodness. Because it comes from within, it is not dependent on others. It is a state of fullness where, as my teacher says, "There is no margin for desires to arise."

True love is for all, not just a few. It does not fluctuate, and so there is no suffering, fear, or loss associated with it. There are no requirements or conditions. It is not a burden placed on someone to sustain our happiness, but rather a treasure we have within that is shared effortlessly with all, at all times. So, love is given, not taken. In a state of love, we are so full we do not need anything from anyone. All neediness has finished and we are truly able to give to everyone.

This is the state we must achieve. To do so, we must look within and check our motives behind what we do, to ensure that whatever we do is done from a place of fullness, rather than of neediness.


*"Love does not cause suffering: what causes it is the sense of ownership, which is love's opposite."*
Antoine de Saint-Exupery

# I - Investigate Your Intentions

I didn't like the word "needy." I had thought I was strong.
She smiled sweetly at me, "Shall we see if I'm wrong?

I'll give you an example to show you where you stand.
Say you open a door and give someone else a hand.

The other walks through without saying, 'Thanks.'
What are you thinking? Don't worry. Be frank."

"I guess it would depend on the state of my mood.
But it's quite likely I'd think, 'Well, that's a bit rude.'"

"Then there is a chance the other may shift your feelings.
You may think ill of him, which affects all future dealings.

But now I will say something, I suspect you will not like.
Check your own intentions. Ask if *you* were doing right.

Sometimes when you help, your motive is well hidden.
It is only revealed when you feel you've been bitten.

So often when you give, you're really looking to take.
You give to fish for love, but no one takes the bait.

When you don't get a catch, you end up feeling sad.
Then you point a finger at the other for being bad.

But what was *your* intention? To take from another.
You did so to feel better, not to give help to the other.

Check if you have the thought, 'I want to help someone else,'
That you do not want to try to help yourself."

This little bit of wisdom went against all I'd been told.
Weren't we meant to help others? Isn't this our role?

I said to the angel, "What kind of world would this make?
So many need help. We must help for goodness sake."

She said, "Listen to what I say, so you will be very clear.
You can help others, but heal yourself first, my dear.

Now you think to give at the expense of the self.
You spend all your energy doing for everyone else.

In truth you are not giving, you're looking for a return.
You want love and appreciation, for this you quietly yearn.

Sadly when you get it, it makes you feel good.
Then you spend your time, not doing what you should.

But the day will come, when you have nothing left to give.
Bitter or depressed you'll think, 'This isn't how to live.'

If you really want to do someone else a favor:
Take care of yourself first. From this, do not waiver.

Then you won't try to take from everything you do.
If you fill the self first, your goodness will shine through.

You'll be ready to give help when someone is in need.
Not just when it's convenient or you want to do a good deed.

Those whom you then help, will not be in your debt.
You won't feel you're helping, but everyone will get.

The secret to achieve this: do everything for God.
Then others need not thank you. He will give the nod.

Your nature is to give. This you were meant to do.
But when you try to take, you're guaranteed to lose.

You'll either become dependent on someone to provide.
Or fear will arise within that you won't be satisfied.

It's better to be a giver. In this you will be free.
It brings peace to the mind and fills the heart with glee.

In order to reach this state, investigate your intentions.
Know why you are doing, on this pay close attention."

Quite often new students say to my teacher, "But isn't this path selfish? It's all about working on the self, on making yourself happy. But what about helping others or making other people happy?" I had similar thoughts when I first began. But now I know this path is about becoming truly selfless, although in the beginning, on the surface, it may seem as though finding happiness within is selfish.

But restoring our happiness is actually the greatest gift we can give, not only to the self, but to others. When we feel happy, we are generous. If we are searching for a parking space and finally find one at the same time as someone else, we let the other person have it and happily continue our search. But when we are running low and our spiritual tank is on empty, then the parking spot is *ours* and woe unto the poor soul who thinks otherwise.

When we are happy, we are not only generous, but allowing and forgiving. We do not take things personally. We can let things go. But when we are not happy, the slightest untoward glance can trigger us to snap, shout, or cry.

Because our happiness depends on others, my teacher regularly suggests doing the following homework assignment. She asks us to keep track of our reactions for one full day. This means every time someone or something brings a reaction in us, whether it is impatience, anger, sadness, disgust, or something else, we write it down. By the end of the day, she says we will have a full account of how needy we are.

I have done this on numerous occasions. But I must confess, I do not always make it through the whole day. By dinner time, my hand is usually cramped from writing, and so I usually stop writing and tell myself I will just remember my reactions, rather than write them down.

This simple exercise is essential, however, if we want to find out how much the rest of the world has control over us. It makes it easy to see how our state of being depends on how others think, speak, and act. By about 10 a.m. it is clear any variations from our own code of conduct, beliefs, or preferences are not tolerated. It is also helpful to reveal our intentions, of which we are sometimes not even aware.

This leads to another piece of homework my teacher often gives. She recommends that no matter what we are doing we ask ourselves, "What is the intention behind what I am doing? Am I doing something because of greed, control, anger, or revenge? Am I trying to teach someone a lesson? Am I sulking to try to punish someone for not doing as I wanted him or her to do? Am I trying to project an image that I am good? Am I trying to please someone? Am I doing something out of duty, commitment, responsibility, or because I need to be needed?"

My teacher often says, "You will know your intentions were not pure when you lose your happiness while doing something for someone." A sign of this is when we think someone is taking advantage of us. If we were honest with ourselves, we would know we did something for someone in the hope of receiving something in return, whether it is love, appreciation, respect, or regard, but failed to receive it. And so, in fact, we were actually trying to take, not give. (The same applies to the thought, "After all I've done for him or her...")

This was a revelation for me to see how often I was taking, when I believed I was giving. I never used to think doing for others was a way of taking for myself. I did not realize the disease to please is not a disease of giving, but rather of taking. It occurs because of the inability to sustain the self and so we do for others so they will give us the love and appreciation we require. And then, when we do not receive what we are looking for, we lose our happiness.

My teacher speaks of four levels of giving that help illustrate this lesson:

1. *I have nothing, so you must give to me.*
   This is the lowest form of giving, which grown children often engage in with their parents.
2. *I will give to you, but you must give to me first.*
   Parents often engage in this with their children, to try to get them to do what they want them to do.
3. *I will give to you, so that you will give to me.*
   This is the most common form of giving today, when we give with an expectation to receive in the future. But then we lose our happiness when we do not receive a return.
4. *I have an abundance and share with everyone.*
   This is the highest form of giving, when there is not even a consciousness of giving. It is when we are so full that our urn is overflowing and then all others receive from us.

We can discover a lot about ourselves and our intentions by exploring these four levels of giving. In the first three, there is an aspect of control and manipulation by the giver, as the giver gives to receive what he or she wants. Often, the giver wants to keep the other dependent on him or her, be it financially or emotionally. In the first three levels, the giver always keeps track and counts what has been given. This is the ego at work. It keeps a close watch on the tally of giving to others. And then when there is a persistent deficit with someone, we lose our happiness. My teacher often says this is a sign we are spiritually bankrupt and our well has run dry.

When we find ourselves in this situation, we need to investigate our intentions, so we can make an adjustment to restore our happiness. Often when we hear someone complain that someone's taking advantage of him or her, the advice others usually give is, "Stop giving." And yes, sometimes my teacher will say this. But she will not leave it at this. She will bring the lesson back to the giver and say, "Why were you over-sustaining that person? Was it because of your need to be needed? Were you trying to control the other?"

Quite often, however, when someone complains that he or she has "given too much," my teacher will say something that makes most of her students, particularly the new ones, shriek with disapproval. She will say, "No, no, you haven't given too much. In fact, you haven't given enough. It is as if you owe that person 1000 rides in your car and you've only given him 15. You have a huge burden of debt with that soul that you need to pay back. But you cannot pay it back with resentment, as you are doing now. You need to do it with happiness. Everything you do must be done with happiness."

The key is our mindset while we do something. If we must do something for someone and resentment is building, we have to shift to stop the resentment. My teacher recommends thinking that God Himself has asked you to do something for one of His children. This helps make us more light-hearted, happy, and willing to do what we must.

When we make a shift, we feel good, so we do good. This contrasts with what I used to do, which was to do good to feel good. But doing good to feel good is not actually doing good. It is doing for the self and no one is served by this, because when we do good to feel good, we use others to sustain ourselves.

The path to happiness is about moving into a place of unlimited love, where giving is natural, a part of who we are. When we give from this place, a place of fullness, then there are no requirements or conditions on others. Whether we receive appreciation, praise, and love, or indifference, scorn, and criticism, it does not matter, because we were not doing to take, we were simply doing, and someone happened to receive. Giving from a pure place guarantees we receive now and later. In this state we are truly selfless.

When we can do this, even just a little bit more each day, the homework assignments become easier. Now, after years of practice, when I write down my reactions my hand still may ache by the end of the day, but I notice there are a lot of things that used to bother me that do not bother me as much, if at all, anymore. So, while I still have a lot of work to do, I know I am making progress. And that is all that matters. I am changing who I am and becoming less dependent on others, which is essential to maintaining my happiness. And when I can sustain myself, then I will be truly selfless.

*"Act with kindness, but don't expect gratitude."*
Confucius

# N – No Desires or Expectations

I could see the wisdom in what she had shared.
And knew within myself, true giving was quite rare.

I always subtly looked to receive what I lacked.
I wanted love and respect and sought it with great tact.

So often I was successful and received what I wanted.
Oh, but when I failed, those moments left me haunted.

I wanted to be free, to give and not to take.
Taking seemed a habit, one I must surely break.

So then I asked the angel, "How can this habit be broken?"
She told me to keep listening to each word that is spoken.

"Taking is the effect, but the cause is desire.
When you are wanting, it's love that you require.

Desires and expectations come when there's no love inside.
Then you search around and hope to be satisfied.

But this is the greatest falsehood. It simply can't be done.
When one desire's satisfied, another will quickly come.

And then you're in a trap, in a spiral going down.
When desires are fulfilled, happiness cannot be found."

"But this isn't what I've heard. It isn't what is taught.
'Chase after your desires' is the prevailing thought."

"A dog chases his tail and you can chase desires.
But will this bring happiness? Or just make you quite tired?

When your desires are met, you'll enjoy a hit of pleasure.
But this isn't happiness. It isn't life's real treasure.

In the shadow of fulfillment lurks the certain fear
That you won't receive, and then there will be tears.

If you're a fortunate soul, your desires won't be satisfied.
Then you'll do the work, to create happiness inside.

When the day comes and your health and wealth are gone,
and all have fallen away, a new day must dawn.

You'll have to stop taking from everything external,
You'll need to turn to God and find something eternal.

Remember that your home isn't here on earth.
It's up above with God, where you recognize your worth.

It is there you'll find the love for which you quietly yearn.
Then you will soon realize life is meant to learn.

And what must you learn? How to sustain yourself.
To stop chasing out there and create your inner wealth.

Please don't waste your time trying to fulfill desires.
Free yourself from them. This is what's required.

You must let things and people be just as they are.
Let go of expectations and I promise you'll go far."

My teacher often says, "You cannot be happy if you have desires." This is because our minds cannot be peaceful, as they are wanting, and our hearts cannot be loving, as they are longing. This obviously contrasts with what we normally hear in the outside world, where our desires are constantly stoked and we are told we will be happy if we can fulfill them.

I have seen the loss that occurs from having desires in my writing. When I wrote with a desire to "save the world," I would become disheartened when I finally finished writing a book and later realized it was not worth sharing. I felt as if people were waiting for a shift to occur and, by not producing something that could make a contribution, I failed on some level.

But writing this book was different. I wrote it to more deeply understand, accept, and practice all I had been learning. Every day I wrote it I felt as if I became better acquainted with myself and moved closer to God. Because of this, I enjoyed writing every page and felt satisfied when I finished it. It did not affect me in the slightest when my pitches to publishers were politely declined. I simply thought the time had not come, they were not the right people to work with, or the book was not meant to be shared.

With this said, I suppose the true test will come in the face of unkind reviews or when people tell me it did not make a difference at all. I realize someone could argue the agenda of this book is the same as my previous books; I have just creatively disguised my desire to "save the world" by trying to convince you to "save yourself... and this will save the world."

This may be true. All I know is that when I used to write, I believe I was writing from a place of anger, as subtle as it might have been. But now, I hope and feel I am writing from a place of love. If this is the case, then no matter what people say about this book, it will be fine, as this book has served its purpose even before it has been printed; it has helped me become better acquainted with myself and God and I am satisfied with that.

In line with this, I heard in class once that "success is bestowed on you by others, but satisfaction arises from within, when you know you have done the best you can." When we strive for satisfaction in what we do and are not dependent on others to bestow success upon us, this is true freedom from desires. If we all strived for inner satisfaction, rather than external success, we would begin to see real progress in the world. It is our desires that ignite the fires that ultimately burn us – both literally in the world and spiritually in our souls.

While the desires that burn the world are obvious, the spiritual ones are not as blatant and may even seem altruistic. We may have a desire for our child to be happy or for our illness or the illness of a loved one to be cured. But these are still desires, which, if not fulfilled, will cause us to lose our happiness. This is not to say that we do not have hope. We must always hope and wish for the best for ourselves and others, but we must understand that whatever anyone experiences is the result of his or her karma, and the outcome depends on that and nothing else.

While I had not considered the loss caused by altruistic desires, I also had not considered the loss from having expecta-tions. It was a revelation to hear that if we have expectations we cannot be happy, particularly because we have so many. Expectations are a form of desire, but they are more subtle and are usually about how other people *should* think, speak, or act.

The moment my teacher hears anyone say "should," she immediately says, "Stop with this word 'should.' Delete it from your vocabulary." Then she explains thinking "should" about anyone or anything is the expressway to unhappiness. "Should" is an expectation, which is the product of each person's condi-tioning, experiences, and beliefs and, therefore, is not necessarily shared by everyone else. So, to think "should" about anyone or anything is an invitation to irritation.

A good example of how "should" can make us lose our happiness is apparent in waiting in line. I grew up in America where we wait in line to be served and now live in England, the birthplace of the queue, where patiently waiting one's turn is sacred. And although I prefer this way of doing things, I have also been to a bank in Asia where I had to jam my passport and currency under the glass more aggressively than the others or I would still be waiting there. If we begin to think everyone *should* wait in line as we do, we will lose our happiness every time someone "jumps the queue."

And so this is the practice, to understand and accept that different people have different ways of doing things. There is no need to take it personally or become upset about it. It is what it is. It will be our turn when it is time. In the meantime, life has brought us an opportunity to practice patience and tolerance – and maybe gentle communication. But in any case, we must maintain our elevated state no matter what others do around us.

My teacher has pointed out most of our "shoulds" are tied to the roles we play: a husband *should* do this, a wife *should* do this, a child *should* do this, a parent *should* do this, a neighbor *should* do this, a religious or spiritual person *should* do this, and someone of a certain nationality or profession *should* do this. And, there is an equally long list in our minds of what everyone should *not* do. All of these "shoulds" and "should nots" put other people in charge of our happiness.

We often have a long list of "shoulds" and "should nots" for our children. I now believe that the list children need to adhere to for their own benefit is actually quite short. However, we usually have a long list of expectations because we often have hidden agendas, as we want our children to promote our sense of self. We want them to be seen as good, polite, smart, or talented by others, so we can then feel good about ourselves.

And so the advice we give is not for their benefit, but for our own.

My teacher, however, recommends giving guidance instead of advice. Guidance is when we share from our experience with the other person's best interest in mind, without having a hidden agenda or an expectation or desire as to whether the guidance is taken or not.

As long as we have desires or expectations, we are in a self-made prison, where everyone else has been appointed warden. If our desires and expectations are fulfilled, then we may enjoy some free time in the yard. But if they are not, then we are back in the dark hole of unhappiness. If, however, we let go of how things "should" be or how people "should" behave, then we are free. No one and nothing can control our state of being. What a glorious state to be in!

*"It is the nature of desire not to be satisfied, and most men live only for the gratification of it."*
Aristotle

# E – Ensure You Observe, Do Not Absorb

"Is there another area that's beneficial to explore?"
"Of course – there are so many. Are you ready to hear more?"

I assured her I was and wondered what was next.
She said it was a good one, not found in many texts.

"When you were little many told you to be nice.
And I have already told you the danger of using vice.

But while it is important to not give another sorrow,
You also mustn't take it, or you'll give it back tomorrow.

Understand this: you can't give what you don't have.
So don't take sorrow, then you won't give what is bad.

You've developed a habit of absorbing what's out there.
You weep when others weep and believe it shows you care.

You think this is a good sign of the compassion you have.
But it's actually just a sign that your heart needs a salve.

It's wounded and broken and aching in pain.
You can't sustain yourself, so you look outside to blame.

So ensure you don't absorb, but instead learn to observe.
If you can learn this art, then everyone will be served.

When you learn to observe, you don't take the outside in.
You protect your love inside, then everybody wins.

In your head you must remember, souls reap what they sow.
And in your heart there must be love, you can't let it run low.

If there is an emptiness, sorrow or anger will fill the space.
Then whatever you feel will show up on your face.

Whether it's sorrow or anger, this you will soon spread.
What you give multiplies, then this burden is on your head.

When other people suffer, they do not need your tears.
When you suffer with them, it only heightens their fears.

They need strength and love to face what it is that's come.
They do not need your weakness. It'll make them want to run.

So don't give pity or anger to those who are in need.
You must give peace and love. This is the better deed.

You can only do this, when your heart's been cured.
Then you won't absorb, but instead you will observe."

I used to be like a giant sponge, absorbing all of the world's sorrow. I would soak up all of the pain and suffering, wring myself out, and then absorb some more. I read so many newspaper articles about terrible things happening everywhere and I would take it all in. Sometimes I would be moved to write a letter, send a check, or donate some clothes. But most of the time I just took it in, felt badly about it, and did nothing but multiply the suffering in the world by repeating what was happening to anyone who cared to listen.

In spite of this, I was still wary about observing and not

absorbing. I was open to observing, because I did not want to feel badly every time I saw the news, but I still resisted the concept. Part of my resistance was simply due to the word "observe." It sounded cold and unfeeling at best, or indifferent at worst. Observing sounded like something a lonely, embittered scientist would do. It certainly did not sound warm, fuzzy, or spiritual. But it was only after learning what it meant to observe that I learned we cannot be truly warm, fuzzy, or spiritual until we learn how to observe.

This is obvious to us in the physical world. When a doctor sees a patient, he or she cannot absorb the pain of the patient. The doctor must observe the patient to give the proper diagnosis. My teacher often jokes, "What if you went to a dentist, opened your mouth to show him an abscess, and then he screamed and passed out? What help could he give you?" Then she explains the same is true in the spiritual world. "You cannot truly help someone who is hurting if you are hurting yourself. Think about it. If you were drowning, would you reach to grab a log that was floating by or a piece of straw?"

When we absorb, we are the piece of straw, unable to be of assistance to anyone. If we meet someone who is angry, we take it personally and it triggers us to become angry. I have heard Dadi Janki say, "Souls are so weak nowadays, most people cannot meet an angry person without becoming angry themselves. But what does an angry person need? More anger? Or peace? We need to be spiritual fire fighters, putting out the fires of anger with the cool water of peace."

In line with this, my teacher recommends looking beyond what is said by others to the meaning behind what is said. She says most of the time people do not say what they actually mean and even more rarely do other people give them what they need.

I practice this often with my daughter. Sometimes when she is irritable or says something unkind, if I realize she did not sleep well the night before then I address her fatigue and not necessarily her words. And if she is a bit clingy, then I know an illness may be brewing and remember this when I respond to her.

The lesson for me in this is to have the love and understanding of a mother with everyone, not just with my daughter. I need to understand there is always an underlying reason why someone is acting a certain way, whether the reason is known or not.

Observing is not just about observing other people or situations, it is also about observing what is happening within; it is an aspect of awareness. For instance, if I am waiting for someone who is late and begin to feel irritated and impatient, I observe that. "Oh, look, here I am becoming irritated and impatient. I am wanting to control what is outside of my control so I can be happy."

Instead of allowing myself to lose my happiness, I can choose to gently generate the "right" kind of thoughts. For instance, I can remember: "But my happiness does not depend on what others do. I have control over myself and do not need to control the outside world. Other people can do as they will. The question is, 'What am I to do in the face of what others have done?' I will use this opportunity to practice patience and tolerance."

And then I can remind myself, "Everything is exactly as it is supposed to be. Everyone is here to help push me toward perfection. The other person will show up when he or she is meant to and not a minute before or after, no matter what I think, say, or do." Then, once he or she arrives, with peace in my mind and love in my heart, I can communicate, if necessary.

As an aside, *other* people are here to push *us* to perfection, by being late or insulting us, but *we* are not here to push *others* to perfection! We need to make sure that our actions do not make others feel irritated or insulted. Therefore, it is best not to keep people waiting or say unkind words about others.

We need to remember the law of karma, that what we think, say, and do comes back to us. So we need to ensure that we only emit goodness and realize when we do not attract goodness, it is because of something we have done at some time. Therefore, do not absorb it. Be thankful to clear that karmic account and let it go.

In truth, understanding and accepting karma is essential to stop absorbing and begin observing. When we know there are no accidents, mistakes, or injustices, then we can greatly reduce, if not eliminate, our suffering in the face of the suffering of others. When we realize that somehow in some way at some time – often unknowingly – a soul has sown the seeds that reaped bitter fruit, then there is nothing to cry about. Whatever is happening is simply a settling of some account and when that account is settled, it is finished. It is only when we look at something in the present without considering the past and future that we suffer.

When we no longer absorb other people's pain and suffering, we can truly be of service to them. We will be able to visit a hospital and not absorb all of the fear, but, rather, radiate love. And we will be able to encounter an angry person and not become angry, but, rather, radiate peace. When we observe and do not absorb, we will be able to radiate peace and love when everyone else is radiating anger and fear. This is one of the greatest gifts we can give to ourselves and others.

*"The one who sees all things and yet rises above them is the one who will walk over the sea."*
Sufi Master Hazrat Inayut Khan

# S - Sit With Yourself and God Everyday

"So please tell me how to cure my aching heart?
What is the secret? Where do I start?"

"The best way to heal is to sit with yourself.
And then sit with God to restore your inner health.

Call it what you will, some will say meditate.
But I can assure you, it's the only way to radiate."

"I've tried to meditate, but don't know what to do.
What is the method? Tell me your view."

"Sit comfortably in a chair and put on a soft song.
Don't be self-conscious or worry you'll do it wrong.

You're just taking time to be with God and yourself,
To leave behind this world, and experience something else.

Much of what I've said has been about thinking and feeling.
But happiness is an experience. It's what you find appealing.

First start with the mind, and gently express peace.
Let the thoughts of this world float away with ease.

See what is lacking within that you want from outside.
Express what it is you need, then you will feel satisfied.

Although you may be lacking the virtues that you need,
When you work to emerge them, God will quickly take heed.

You'll feel a wave of power or a warm burst of love,
And you may just experience your soul's gone up above.

You're no longer of this body. You're no longer of this earth.
You're in the presence of God and restore your self worth.

You have access to the wisdom lying latent within you.
You have clarity of mind and know what you should do.

This love that envelopes you, gives security and belonging.
You'll no longer be so needy, chasing others and fawning."

"But what if this doesn't happen? What if I feel nothing?
What if my mind isn't peaceful and my heart isn't loving?"

"Then the chances are high you won't try for very long.
You'll feel anxious or bored and think you're doing it wrong.

You'll find every excuse not to sit and meditate.
You'll get lost in doing, but for being you'll hesitate."

Then the angel spoke gently, to show me what to do.
Through her loving words, I experienced something new.

My mind became quiet and I experienced pure silence.
I was filled with peace, in a state of non-violence.

My thoughts suspended, I had no worries or desires.
The flicker of love within spread like a wild fire.

When I came down, I was buzzing with delight.
I had a new awareness: I am a point of light.

I am not my body. I am separate from it.
Limited roles and labels simply did not fit.

My awareness expanded. I could see more than I was able.
Now I could see the tree, in what had been just a table.

But beyond just this, I could see there'd be a day
When that table would crumble and begin to decay.

The material world could no longer pull me.
The eternal I wanted, what would always be.

"Sit with yourself and God to bring goodness to the soul.
And then happiness becomes a much simpler goal."

I must admit I only began meditating regularly a few years after beginning to take classes at The Spiritual University. Initially, I loved the wisdom and it improved my state of being so much that I did not feel the need to meditate.

Of course, I tried it initially, as my teacher spoke of such glorious states that could be achieved in meditation. But I quickly lost interest when I did not experience my own inner fireworks, but rather just saw my mind generate an endless series of mundane thoughts.

But then I reached a point where I felt I was not progressing. The same things affected me and I felt I needed to increase my effort. I had no other choice. I had to try meditation.

Up until that point, most of my effort was in my head, in trying to think the "right" thoughts. But meditation is about engaging the heart and truly transforming who you are, not consciously through an effort, but deep down within, below the surface of consciousness.

Although there are many different forms of meditation and everyone has to find the one that works for them, Raja Yoga Meditation, as taught by The Spiritual University, appealed to me because its philosophy seemed to make sense. The translation of "Raja Yoga Meditation" best describes what it is and what it does. "Raja" means "king" or "supreme" and "yoga" means "union," while "meditation" is probably derived from the same root as the Latin word *mederi*, which means "to heal." So, by coming into union with God, or connecting with God, you heal yourself.

My teacher points out Raja Yoga Meditation differs from most other meditative practices as it is about fullness of mind, rather than emptiness of mind, which is often the stated goal of meditation. But I believe, as my teacher says, that what we want is to channel the *power* of the mind, not *empty* the mind. An empty mind will not transform someone, but a powerful mind will.

Beyond this, my teacher also describes meditation as a way of being, not something we do. It is a state of introversion, of connection to the goodness we have within, so we can connect to something greater. When this state is achieved, then it is as if we have plugged our soul into the ultimate battery charger and we can experience and fill ourselves with the limitless supply of virtue God has and transform our old nature into a divine one.

The practice of meditation is, at least in theory, very simple. I say, "in theory," because the methodology is simple, but our minds are undisciplined, so it can often take weeks, months, or even years to begin to glimpse the beautiful states described by those who are experienced in meditation.

First of all, I sit comfortably and, as my teacher recommends, I "close the doors on the elevator" so I can ascend. I need to pull the energy of my senses inward, look within, and remember who I am. Then, as various thoughts from the outside world float into my mind and try to distract me, I gently let them go and bring my mind back to remembering who I am, that I am a soul.

Once I have stabilized myself in this, I can do or experience many things. I can think deeply about some point of wisdom from a class or a book and explore it in depth. I can receive clarity on what I need to do in a certain situation or with a certain person. I can experience periods of silence, where the constant chatter I am used to hearing in my mind suspends. I can experience a wave of peace, love, or power. I can experience being in God's presence. And, I can experience my soul as being separate from my body. Beyond this, many have visions of the past or the future.

With this said, probably the biggest barrier to my meditation, at least initially, was expectation. I had grand visions of being a detached yogi meditating on a mountain top. But when I sat to meditate, all I could think of were grocery lists and birthday parties. Soon, all I felt was a mixture of boredom, discomfort, and frustration.

In spite of this, I kept at it. And every time I tried to let go of what I had to do, what I had said and done that day, what others had said and done, and on and on. And I just tried to redirect my mind to remember who I was.

And then one day, it happened. My mind went quiet and I experienced what I can only describe as an elevated sense of being, a fullness within. And then I knew I could do it. At least on some level, I could meditate. Then it became a matter of practicing to be able to return to that state, to experience that feeling, and strengthen it so I could sustain it, no matter what I was doing.

Sometimes, I am able to quickly switch into this state and experience this inner fullness just by pulling my attention inward and remembering who I am. On some occasions I feel as if I have gone beyond time. I feel as though I only sat to meditate for a few minutes, but then discover that 30 to 45 minutes have actually passed. During these times in particular, I feel as though I have left this world behind and have been in the presence of God. And after I come down, I feel incredibly blessed.

This is not to say I do not still struggle meditating. Sometimes I cannot pull my attention inward, usually because I have been pulled by the outside world – by people or circumstances or desires. In this state, I cannot experience a state of being or introversion and then I feel far, far away from God.

The goal is to always be in a state of introversion, of inner fulfillment and connection with God, no matter who I am with or what I am doing. And then life becomes a walking meditation, whether I am cooking, cleaning, or working, I am in a state of inner fulfillment. To do this, I need to keep my attention on the self and work on building a connection, a relationship with God.

In this state, I know who I am, a soul and not a body. Then I can move from the limited thoughts of my body into the unlimited experience of my soul. In the limited, I have love for a few, am mortal, and therefore feel fear and anxiety. In the unlimited, I have love for all, am eternal, and am fearless and carefree.

There are so many beautiful accounts of near death experiences where people experience their souls as being separate from their bodies. Many experience going toward a light and feeling the intense love of God. Most people who come back from this experience are changed and determined to live in a more loving and giving way.

We need not wait for our physical hearts to stop to experience this bliss. All we need to do is learn to quiet our minds, nurture the love that lies latent within us, let go of all desires and expectations – particularly for an experience in meditation – and let God do the rest.

The Spiritual University has published a number of books that explain Raja Yoga Meditation in depth. Each one shares the necessary points of wisdom, as well as the methodology, to be able to begin meditating on a daily basis. Some come with CDs and written thoughts for meditation, which describe how we may gently guide our thoughts in meditation. An example of how to guide our thoughts is:

*Sitting quietly, I bring my attention inward...*
*I allow my body to relax, to let go of all stress and tension...*
*I allow my mind to let go of everything that has happened before this moment...*
*Gently, I come into the present moment...*
*In this serene atmosphere, I remember who I am...*
*A being of peace...*
*Whereas before I used to search for peace in nature, now I know I am peace...*
*I... am... peace...*
*I sustain this thought of peace, of being peace, and begin to feel it...*
*This feeling expands within me to become an experience...*
*I feel a natural detachment from this physical world...*
*I feel calm and content...*
*This is who I am, who I am meant to be...*
*This feeling of peace and serenity is my true nature...*
*I sit quietly and enjoy this experience of being a peaceful soul...*

Once we experience our original nature, a being of peace, the last and final step to restore our happiness occurs naturally.

*"To become like the Father means that whatever qualities, virtues, and powers God has, He gives them to us."*
Dadi Janki

## S - Soar With Gratitude

Learning all that I had, I was grateful God sent her.
I wanted to give thanks, for His angelic cure.

I asked if I could thank God for sending her to me.
"Yes, of course, you can. Say, 'Thank you,' as you please.

Gratitude is essential, if you want to soar.
But even in being thankful, I must say a little more.

Check if you blame whenever things go wrong.
But then when things go well, you sing a different song.

So many just say, 'Thanks,' when they have received.
But why not be grateful, even when you've been deceived?

When you feel insulted or even a little hurt,
Some sweet soul has come to help you in your work.

The other soul has shown you, what work is left for you.
Only then can you realize what you need to do.

Somehow in some way, you tried to take from outside.
So you must be grateful, for the reminder to look inside.

When challenges arrive, thank God for the strength to face.
It's only through this, that your greatness you will taste.

How will you ever know what capacity you have,
If everything goes your way and life is simply fab?"

I agreed with what she said, but had to ask a question.
"And when things go well? What is your suggestion?"

"Be sure that you give thanks when you reap sweet fruit.
Do not to take full credit and give God the boot.

Of course your good fortune comes from your own actions.
But thinking in this way will bring up ego reactions!

You'll start to take support from what has come your way.
And then you'll be so sad, when it all falls away.

You must realize God made your conscience awaken.
This made you do well, so He shouldn't be forsaken.

If you want to thank Him, become who you were meant to be.
Return to your original state, a state of divinity.

When you do this charity and truly heal yourself,
You'll heal this broken world and serve everyone else."

Just hearing these words, made me soar with gratitude.
My hope had been restored. I had a brand new attitude.

I had been given the wisdom and shown the simple way
To learn how to be happy, each and every day.

I first learned I could soar with gratitude when I started keeping
a gratitude journal after reading *Simple Abundance* by Sarah Ban
Breathnach. The recommendation was simple and yet powerful.
Every day I had to write five things for which I was grateful. That

was it. And yet, within a few weeks, by focusing throughout the day on finding a few things for which to be grateful at the end of the day, the quality of my entire day changed.

I did this diligently for four years. Now, when I review my journals and read what I was thankful for, I see that while I had gratitude for the pleasures in life – like a good meal or a beautiful sunset – much of what I was thankful for was simply the joy of being alive. I was thankful for everyone I was fortunate enough to know at home or at work and also for all of the revelations I was having about myself and life through my reading and writing.

What is more interesting to me, however, are the things for which I did not give thanks. Although I had a piece of art hanging in my home that reminded me to "Give thanks for *everything*," I did not give thanks for the challenges in life. I had gratitude for having my desires fulfilled, for people treating me with respect, and for things going my way. But I did not give thanks when things did not turn out as I wanted them to and I ended up feeling humiliated, insulted, disappointed, hurt, or sad. Now I understand it is in the midst of challenges – when we feel the greatest upheaval – that we have the greatest opportunity to learn and grow.

My teacher, who has faced many challenges throughout her life, said Dadi Janki once told her, "Tests come that are just a bit beyond our capacity so we'll expand our capacity in facing them." My teacher also says she expresses gratitude for all that happens, because she knows she is being pushed to perfection with each test. Giving thanks is also a way of blessing a situation and removing any influence or power it may have over your state of being.

If I were to keep a gratitude journal now, while I would still give thanks for family and friends, I suspect many of my entries would be quite different. I would give thanks to God, for giving me the wisdom to enable me to help myself. I would give thanks for attracting a great teacher, who pushes me to be better and do better. I would give thanks for the challenges in life, because I know everything I face will only make me more experienced and stronger. I would give thanks for the times when things did not go my way, when someone did not speak to me as I would have wanted or something did not happen as I expected, as it inspires me to keep coming to class and not reduce my effort.

I would give thanks for having enough faith, courage, and love to make an effort each day to reach that glorious state where my happiness depends on no one and nothing. I would give thanks for those moments when I see the highest vision of myself – and others. I would give thanks for every revelation I had that enabled me to transform myself.

I would give thanks for The Spiritual University, the founders, leaders, teachers, and students, who have lived or continue to live their lives with the aim of becoming completely peaceful and loving at all times with all people. I would give thanks to God for bringing me into a place filled with benevolent men and women who are dedicated to serving humanity. And I would give thanks for the hope and belief burning within me that simply by changing ourselves we can change the world.

I could continue writing and writing about all the things for which I am grateful. Just writing that list makes me soar even higher. The best part is that most of what I am now grateful for cannot be taken away from me. Before, my gratitude was often for what was perishable, but now my gratitude is for what is eternal. No one can take away the wisdom I have learned; the love I have found within; and the hope, faith, and courage I now have. And for this, I am eternally grateful.

Interestingly, learning to give thanks marked the beginning of my spiritual journey. In truth, it is the beginning *and* the end. If we do not have gratitude for being, which is love for the self, we will not be able to be grateful for anything or anyone. And without gratitude, we cannot find happiness, because our hearts have shut down. In this state, we will not be able to make the effort, keep attention on the self, and work every day to free ourselves from our suffering.

But if you have made it this far in this book, it shows that you have at least a drop of love for yourself. And with wisdom and practice, you can turn that drop into an ocean of love for yourself, God, and everyone else. Then, no one and nothing will be able to take your happiness away.

*"Gratitude is not only the greatest of virtues, but the parent of all others."*
Cicero

# The Angel Departs

The angel then said, "It's time for me to go.
I've told you enough of what you need to know.

Now you need to practice, to make it your own.
Work with the wisdom and let go of what you've known.

Remember what I said? That your purpose is to be happy?
You didn't believe me and thought it was a bit sappy.

While I spoke the truth, happiness isn't only for you.
It's radiated to others in everything you do.

Finding happiness within is the most charitable gift.
It affects everyone on earth and has the power to uplift.

Then you become the angel and spread this happiness to all.
But don't do it with your words. This will be your downfall.

Just be the example. Demonstrate what you know.
Then all will come running, wondering why you glow.

Be sure to do the work and take responsibility for yourself.
Don't search outside or depend on someone else.

Practice using the wisdom to restore your peace of mind.
And open up your heart; learn to be loving and truly kind.

You must reach the state where nothing disturbs your peace,
You're loving and benevolent. This effort must not cease.

But don't become disheartened. You will go up and down.
Just keep finding the smile that's hiding behind the frown.

Success is not measured in being happy all the time.
It's reducing the time to recover and be fine.

When you endeavor to do this, you'll be doing God's work.
You'll bring heaven back onto this spinning earth.

Oh, if you only knew how much God needs you
To transform yourself and make this world brand new."

Then the angel flew away, without looking back.
I knew in that moment, I must give myself what I lack.

So I made a promise to restore my peace of mind,
And learn how to truly love, so happiness will be mine.

This will be my gift, I give just to myself.
But the beauty of it is, it's shared with everyone else.

It is time for me to say, "Goodbye," too. But before I finish, I
would like to pass on my teacher's insight into the journey to
happiness: "It is like the game of *Snakes and Ladders*. You can
climb all the way up to 99, get bitten – usually by your ego – and
then slide all the way back to the beginning again."

I do not wish to scare you, but rather to prepare you. When
we start working on ourselves, we experience some achieve-
ments to encourage us. My teacher says this is so we can say
"those three magical words, 'I did it.'" But she is quick to
caution, "Take the achievement, but renounce the arrogance

over the achievement. If you become arrogant about what you've achieved, everyone you know will line up around the block to test you tomorrow."

But there will also be times when we do not achieve. It has happened to all of us. We float out of a class one day and say, "I'm going to be so peaceful and loving to everyone always," and then the next person we see presses our buttons and we erupt with the force of Mt. Etna. Or, if we do not explode, we may absorb some sadness from the outside, stew in negativity about someone or something, or become impatient or intolerant. In any event, our minds are not at peace and our hearts are not loving.

During these times, we must not beat ourselves up or allow ourselves to become disheartened. We need to stop and see what was at the root of the problem and work through the ART of Awareness, Realization, and Transformation. Once we have a realization and make a shift within, then we can let go of what has happened, and begin anew. When my happiness reduces, I return to the practice of HAPPINESS and ask myself these questions to work my way through the ART:

H - **Have the "right" thoughts** (What is the quality of my thoughts? Have I forgotten: Who I am? Who I belong to? Why things happen? What I am meant to be doing? And that there is benefit in everything?)

A - **Awareness of the self** (Am I thinking about what others *should* be doing? What do I need to do in the face of what the other has done? What is happening within me? Am I not seeing the highest vision of myself or others?)

P - **Possess self-respect, not ego** (Am I resisting what is? Am I reacting and not responding? Am I trying to teach someone a lesson or seeking revenge? Am I comparing? Competing? Criticizing? Condemning? Trying to control the uncontrollable?

Am I giving respect?)

**P - Prefer no one, love all** (Am I loving in limited terms, preferring my own over others? Am I forgetting everyone is a child of God and therefore my sibling? Am I keeping my heart from loving by hanging onto past hurt when I need to let go?)

**I - Investigate your intentions** (Have I been trying to take when I am meant to give? Have I been trying to control – either overtly or covertly through pleasing – to receive what I want? Have I done out of duty, responsibility, obligation or guilt?)

**N - No desires or expectations** (What did I want that I failed to receive? Why am I linking my happiness to something outside of my control?)

**E - Ensure you observe, do not absorb** (Have I forgotten the law of karma, that we reap what we sow? Is there a karmic account at play? Do I want this person or situation to have control over me?)

**S - Sit with yourself and God** (Have I been chasing after others and not after God? Have I been looking after myself and taking time for reflection and nurturing the self?)

**S - Soar with gratitude** (Have I forgotten everything for which I have to be grateful?)

With that, I wish you the best in bringing peace back into your mind and love into your heart. Happiness is your birthright. You are meant to have peace of mind and love in your heart in all situations with all people. So, no matter what happens, do not ever give up. You can do it. You will do it.

Everyone on earth is waiting for you to restore your

happiness. Give this gift to yourself. It will be the most incredible gift you have ever been given, and in turn, it is automatically given to others. It is only by changing ourselves that we can change the world. When you change yourself, then you become an angel, an angel that is doing God's work by bringing peace and love back onto this earth.

*"To put the world right in order, we must first put the nation in order; to put the nation in order, we must first put the family in order; to put the family in order, we must first cultivate our personal life; we must first set our hearts right."*
Confucius

# About the Angel

Gizi Pruthi, a widely travelled and gifted spiritual teacher, is the "angel who whispered". For more than 20 years she has practiced and taught meditation with The Brahma Kumaris World Spiritual University and coordinates the activities of one of their centers in London. She regularly conducts lectures, retreats, and self-empowerment groups and has inspired many to bring positive change in their lives. After a successful business career in India and the UK, she settled in London. She is married and has two sons.

# About the Author

Patricia Tashiro has a Masters Degree in International Relations and has come to believe, while studying with Giziben, that peace, love, and happiness will only come in the world when we find it within. *An Angel Whispered* provides the wisdom and practical method to do so. Married, with a child, she lives in London.

# BOOKS

O is a symbol of the world, of oneness and unity. In different cultures it also means the "eye," symbolizing knowledge and insight. We aim to publish books that are accessible, constructive and that challenge accepted opinion, both that of academia and the "moral majority."

Our books are available in all good English language bookstores worldwide. If you don't see the book on the shelves ask the bookstore to order it for you, quoting the ISBN number and title. Alternatively you can order online (all major online retail sites carry our titles) or contact the distributor in the relevant country, listed on the copyright page.

See our website www.o-books.net for a full list of over 500 titles, growing by 100 a year.

And tune in to myspiritradio.com for our book review radio show, hosted by June-Elleni Laine, where you can listen to the authors discussing their books.

MySpiritRadio